Contents

Foreword

This book is not a collection of hitherto unpublished work, it is a collection of essays which are not presently in print but which Murray White of HarperCollins and myself think should remain available to the reading public. One of the legacies which one inherits from a great writer is the responsibility to try to ensure that his minor works do not vanish from publication, or at the very least that they do not vanish until people no longer want to read them.

In this volume, we have tried to select those essays of Jack's (C. S. Lewis) which are applicable to today's world and still very much in demand. Jack said that a writer should not try to be 'modern' or 'up to date' because the more that he achieves it, the more he ensures that in a very short time he will be 'out of date'. And it is this ability to achieve timelessness which so characterizes the best of Jack's essays and articles. It is inevitable that some of what Jack wrote is coloured and affected by his upbringing and the environment in which he lived, but the crystal clarity of his thinking frequently enabled him to cut through the shrouds of his era and reach to the very heart of matters which will concern men and women of thought for all time. We hope that you will find this phenomenon explained in this book.

Douglas Gresham
Ireland 1996

Compelling Reason

Essays on Ethics and Theology

C. S. Lewis
Edited by Walter Hooper

Fount
An Imprint of HarperCollinsPublishers

Fount Paperbacks is an Imprint of
HarperCollins*Religious*
Part of HarperCollins*Publishers*
77–85 Fulham Palace Road, London W6 8JB

The material in this compilation was previously published in:

First and Second Things, first published in *Undeceptions* by Geoffrey Bles, London 1971; first
Fount Paperback edition published in 1985. (Essays 2, 3, 6, 10, 13, 15, 16, 18, 21)
Copyright © 1985 C. S. Lewis Pte Ltd

Present Concerns, first published in 1986 by Fount Paperbacks. (Essays 4, 5, 7, 8, 9, 11, 17, 22, 23)
Copyright © 1986 C. S. Lewis Pte Ltd

Timeless At Heart, first published in 1987 by Fount Paperbacks. (Essays 1, 12, 14, 19, 20, 24)
Copyright © 1970, 1980, 1987 C. S. Lewis Pte Ltd

This edition first published in Great Britain
in 1996 by Fount Paperbacks

1 3 5 7 9 10 8 6 4 2

Copyright © 1996 C. S. Lewis Pte Ltd
Foreword Copyright © 1996 C.S. Lewis Pte. Ltd

A catalogue record for this book is
available from the British Library

0 00 628011 0

Printed and bound in Great Britain by
Caledonian International Book Manufacturing Ltd, Glasgow

1 Why I Am Not a Pacifist (1940)

The question is whether to serve in the wars at the command of the civil society to which we belong is a wicked action, or an action morally indifferent, or an action morally obligatory. In asking how to decide this question, we are raising a much more general question: how do we decide what is good or evil? The usual answer is that we decide by conscience. But probably no one thinks now of conscience as a separate faculty, like one of the senses. Indeed, it cannot be so thought of. For an autonomous faculty like a sense cannot be argued with; you cannot argue a man into seeing green if he sees blue. But the conscience can be altered by argument; and if you did not think so, you would not have asked me to come and argue with you about the morality of obeying the civil law when it tells us to serve in the wars. Conscience, then, means the whole man engaged in a particular subject matter.

But even in this sense conscience still has two meanings. It can mean (a) the pressure a man feels upon his will to do what he thinks is right; (b) his judgement as to what the content of right and wrong are. In sense (a) conscience is always to be followed. It is the sovereign of the universe, which 'if it had power as it has right, would absolutely rule the world'. It is not to be argued with, but obeyed, and even to question it is to incur guilt. But in sense (b) it is a very different matter. People may be mistaken about wrong and right; most people in some degree are mistaken. By what means are mistakes in this field to be corrected?

The most useful analogy here is that of Reason – by which I do not mean some separate faculty but, once more, the whole man judging, only judging this time not about good and evil, but about truth and falsehood. Now any concrete train of reasoning involves three elements.

Firstly, there is the reception of facts to reason about. These facts are received either from our own senses, or from the report of other minds; that is, either experience or authority supplies us with our material. But each man's experience is so limited that the second source is the more usual; of every hundred facts upon which to reason, ninety-nine depend on authority.

Secondly, there is the direct, simple act of the mind perceiving self-evident truth, as when we see that if A and B both equal C, then they equal each other. This act I call intuition.

Thirdly, there is an art or skill of arranging the facts so as to yield a series of such intuitions which linked together produce a proof of the truth or falsehood of the proposition we are considering. Thus in a geometrical proof each step is seen by intuition, and to fail to see it is to be not a bad geometrician but an idiot. The skill comes in arranging the material into a series of intuitable 'steps'. Failure to do this does not mean idiocy, but only lack of ingenuity or invention. Failure to follow it need not mean idiocy, but either inattention or a defect of memory which forbids us to hold all the intuitions together.

Now all correction of errors in reasoning is really correction of the first or the third element. The second, the intuitional element, cannot be corrected if it is wrong, nor supplied if it is lacking. You can give the man new facts. You can invent a simpler proof, that is, a simpler concatenation of intuitable truths. But when you come to an absolute inability to see any one of the self-evident steps out of which the proof is built, then you can do nothing. No doubt this absolute inability is much rarer than we suppose. Every teacher knows that people are constantly protesting that they 'can't see' some self-evident inference, but the supposed inability is usually a refusal to see, resulting either from some passion which *wants* not to see the truth in question or else from sloth which does not want to think at all. But when the inability is real, argument is at an end. You cannot produce rational intuition by argument, because argument depends upon rational intuition. Proof rests upon the unprovable which has to be just 'seen'. Hence faulty intuition is incorrigible. It does not follow that it cannot be trained by practice in attention and in the mortification of disturbing passions, or corrupted by the opposite habits. But it is not amenable to correction by argument.

Before leaving the subject of Reason, I must point out that authority not only combines with experience to produce the raw material, the 'facts', but also has to be frequently used instead of reasoning itself as a method of getting conclusions. For example, few of us have followed the reasoning on which even ten percent of the truths we believe are based. We accept them on authority from the experts and are wise to do so, for though we are thereby sometimes deceived, yet we should have to live like savages if we did not.

Now all three elements are found also in conscience. The facts, as before, come from experience and authority. I do not mean 'moral facts' but those facts about actions without holding which we could not raise moral questions at all – for we should not even be discussing Pacifism if we did not know what war and killing meant, nor Chastity, if we had not yet learned what schoolmasters used to call 'the facts of life'. Secondly, there are the pure intuitions of utterly simple good and evil as such. Third, there is the process of argument by which you arrange the intuitions so as to convince a man that a particular act is wrong or right. And finally, there is authority as a substitute for argument, telling a man of some wrong or right which he would not otherwise have discovered, and rightly accepted if the man has good reason to believe the authority wiser and better than

3

himself. The main difference between Reason and Conscience is an alarming one. It is thus: that while the unarguable intuitions on which all depend are liable to be corrupted by passion when we are considering truth and falsehood, they are much more liable, they are almost certain to be corrupted when we are considering good and evil. For then we are concerned with some action to be here and now done or left undone by ourselves. And we should not be considering that action at all unless we had some wish either to do or not to do it, so that in this sphere we are bribed from the very beginning. Hence the value of authority in checking, or even superseding, our own activity is much greater in this sphere than in that of Reason. Hence, too, human beings must be trained in obedience to the moral intuitions almost before they have them, and years before they are rational enough to discuss them, or they will be corrupted before the time for discussion arrives.

These basic moral intuitions are the only element in Conscience which cannot be argued about; if there can be a difference of opinion which does not reveal one of the parties as a moral idiot, then it is not an intuition. They are the ultimate preferences of the will for love rather than hatred, and happiness rather than misery. There are people so corrupted as to have lost even these, just as there are people who can't see the simplest proof, but in the main these can be said to be the voice of humanity as such. And they are unarguable. But here the trouble begins. People are constantly claiming this unarguable and unanswerable status for moral judgements which are not really intuitions at all but remote consequences or particular applications of them, eminently open to discussion since the consequences may be illogically drawn or the application falsely made.

Thus you may meet a 'temperance' fanatic who claims to have an unanswerable intuition that all strong drink is forbidden. Really he can have nothing of the sort. The real intuition is that health and harmony are good. Then there is a generalization from facts to the effect that drunkenness produces disease and quarrelling, and perhaps also, if the fanatic is Christian, the voice of Authority saying that the body is the temple of the Holy Ghost. Then there is a conclusion that what can always be abused had better never be used at all – a conclusion eminently suited for discussion. Finally, there is the process whereby early associations, arrogance, and the like turn the remote conclusion into something which the man thinks unarguable because he does not wish to argue about it.

This, then is our first canon for moral decisions. Conscience in the (a) sense, the thing that moves us to do right, has absolute authority, but conscience in the (b) sense, our judgement as to what is right, is a mixture of inarguable intuitions and highly arguable processes of reasoning or of submission to authority; and nothing is to be treated as an intuition unless it is such that no good man has ever dreamed of doubting. The man who 'just feels' that total abstinence from drink or marriage is obligatory is to be treated like the man who 'just feels sure' that *Henry VIII* is not by Shakespeare, or that vaccination does no good. For a mere unargued conviction is in place only when we are dealing with the axiomatic; and these views are not axiomatic.

I therefore begin by ruling out one Pacifist position which probably no one present holds, but which conceivably might be held – that of the man who claims to know on the ground of immediate intuition that all killing of human beings is in all circumstances an absolute evil. With the man who reaches the same result by reasoning or authority, I can argue. Of the man who claims not to reach it but to start there, we can only say that he can have no such intuition as he claims. He is mistaking an opinion, or, more likely, a passion, for an intuition. Of course, it would be rude to say this to him. *To* him we can only say that if he is not a moral idiot, then unfortunately the rest of the human

5

race, including its best and wisest, are, and that argument across such a chasm is impossible.

Having ruled out this extreme case, I return to enquire how we are to decide on a question of morals. We have seen that every moral judgement involves facts, intuition and reasoning, and, if we are wise enough to be humble, it will involve some regard for authority as well. Its strength depends on the strength of these four factors. Thus if I find that the facts on which I am working are clear and little disputed, that the basic intuition is unmistakably an intuition, that the reasoning which connects this intuition with the particular judgement is strong, and that I am in agreement or (at worst) not in disagreement with authority, then I can trust my moral judgement with reasonable confidence. And if, in addition, I find little reason to suppose that any passion has secretly swayed my mind, this confidence is confirmed. If, on the other hand, I find the facts doubtful, the supposed intuition by no means obvious to all good men, the reasoning weak, and authority against me, then I ought to conclude that I am probably wrong. And if the conclusion which I have reached turns out also to flatter some strong passion of my own, then my suspicion should deepen into moral certainty. By 'moral certainty' I mean that degree of certainty proper to moral decisions; for mathematical certainty is not here to be looked for. I now apply these tests to the judgement, 'It is immoral to obey when the civil society of which I am a member commands me to serve in the wars!'

First as to the facts. The main relevant fact admitted by all parties is that war is very disagreeable. The main contention urged as fact by pacifists would be that wars always do more harm than good. How is one to find out whether this is true? It belongs to a class of historical generalizations which involve a comparison between the actual consequences of some actual event and a consequence which might have followed if that event had not occurred. 'Wars do no good' involves the proposition

6

that if the Greeks had yielded to Xerxes and the Romans to Hannibal, the course of history ever since would have been perhaps better, but certainly no worse than it actually has been; that a Mediterranean world in which Carthaginian power succeeded Persian would have been at least as good and happy and as fruitful for all posterity as the actual Mediterranean world in which Roman power succeeded Greek. My point is not that such an opinion seems to me overwhelmingly improbable. My point is that both opinions are merely speculative; there is no conceivable way of convincing a man of either. Indeed it is doubtful whether the whole conception of 'what would have happened' – that is, of unrealized possibilities – is more than an imaginative technique for giving a vivid rhetorical account of what did happen.

That wars do no good is then so far from being a fact that it hardly ranks as a historical opinion. Nor is the matter mended by saying 'modern wars'; how are we to decide whether the total effect would have been better or worse if Europe had submitted to Germany in 1914? It is, of course, true that wars never do half the good which the leaders of the belligerents say they are going to do. Nothing ever does half the good – perhaps nothing ever does half the evil – which is expected of it. And that may be a sound argument for not pitching one's propaganda too high. But it is no argument against war. If a Germanized Europe in 1914 would have been an evil, then the war which prevented that evil was, so far, justified. To call it useless because it did not also cure slums and unemployment is like coming up to a man who has just succeeded in defending himself from a man-eating tiger and saying, 'It's no good, old chap. This hasn't really cured your rheumatism!'

On the test of the fact, then, I find the Pacifist position weak. It seems to me that history is full of useful wars as well as of useless wars. If all that can be brought against the frequent appearance of utility is mere speculation about what could have happened, I am not converted.

I turn next to the intuition. There is no question of discussion once we have found it; there is only the danger of mistaking for an intuition something which is really a conclusion and therefore needs argument. We want something which no good man has ever disputed; we are in search of platitude. The relevant intuition seems to be that love is good and hatred bad, or that helping is good and harming bad.

We have next to consider whether reasoning leads us from this intuition to the Pacifist conclusion or not. And the first thing I notice is that intuition can lead to no action until it is limited in some way or other. You cannot do *simply* good to *simply* Man; you must do this or that good to this or that man. And if you do *this* good, you can't at the same time do *that;* and if you do it to *these* men, you can't also do it to *those.* Hence from the outset the law of beneficence involves not doing some good to some men at some times. Hence those rules which so far as I know have never been doubted, as that we should help one we have promised to help rather than another, or a benefactor rather than one who has no special claims on us, or a compatriot more than a stranger, or a kinsman rather than a mere compatriot. And this in fact most often means helping A at the expense of B, who drowns while you pull A on board. And sooner or later, it involves helping A by actually doing some degree of violence to B. But when B is up to mischief against A, you must either do nothing (which disobeys the intuition) or you must help one against the other. And certainly no one's conscience tells him to help B, the guilty. It remains, therefore, to help A. So far, I suppose, we all agree. If the argument is not to end in an anti-Pacifist conclusion, one or other of two stopping places must be selected. You must either say that violence to B is lawful only if it stops short of killing, or else that killing of individuals is indeed lawful but the mass killing of a war is not.

As regards the first, I admit the general proposition that the lesser violence done to B is always preferable to the greater, provided that it is equally efficient in restraining him and equally good for everyone concerned, including B, whose claim is inferior to all the other claims involved but not nonexistent. But I do not therefore conclude that to kill B is always wrong. In some instances — for instance in a small, isolated community, death may be the only efficient method of restraint. In any community its effect on the population, not simply as a deterrent through fear, but also as an expression of the moral importance of certain crimes, may be valuable. And as for B himself, I think a bad man is at least as likely to make a good end in the execution shed some weeks after the crime as in the prison hospital twenty years later. I am not producing arguments to show that capital punishment is certainly right; I am only maintaining that it is not certainly wrong; it is a matter on which good men may legitimately differ.

As regards the second, the position seems to be much clearer. It is arguable that a criminal can always be satisfactorily dealt with without the death penalty. It is certain that a whole nation cannot be prevented from taking what it wants except by war. It is almost equally certain that the absorption of certain societies by certain other societies is a greater evil. The doctrine that war is always a great evil seems to imply a materialist ethic, a belief that death and pain are the greatest evils. But I do not think they are. I think the suppression of a higher religion by a lower, or even a higher secular culture by a lower, a much greater evil. Nor am I greatly moved by the fact that many of the individuals we strike down in war are innocent. That seems, in a way, to make war not worse but better. All men die, and most men miserably. That two soldiers on opposite sides, each believing his own country to be in the right, each at the moment when his selfishness is most in abeyance and his will to sacrifice in the ascendant, should kill each other in plain battle seems to me by no means one of the most terrible things in this very terrible world. Of

9

course, one of them (at least) must be mistaken. And of course war is a very great evil. But that is not the question. The question is whether war is the greatest evil in the world, so that any state of affairs which might result from submission is certainly preferable. And I do not see any really cogent arguments for that view.

Another attempt to get a Pacifist conclusion from the intuition is of a more political and calculating kind. If not the greatest evil, yet war is a great evil. Therefore, we should all like to remove it if we can. But every war leads to another war. The removal of war must therefore be attempted. We must increase by propaganda the number of Pacifists in each nation until it becomes great enough to deter that nation from going to war. This seems to me wild work. Only liberal societies tolerate Pacifists. In the liberal society, the number of Pacifists will either be large enough to cripple the state as a belligerent, or not. If not, you have done nothing. If it is large enough, then you have handed over the state which does tolerate Pacifists to its totalitarian neighbour who does not. Pacifism of this kind is taking the straight road to a world in which there will be no Pacifists.

It may be asked whether, faint as the hope is of abolishing war by Pacifism, there is any other hope. But the question belongs to a mode of thought which I find quite alien to me. It consists in assuming that the great permanent miseries in human life must be curable if only we can find the right cure; and it then proceeds by elimination and concludes that whatever is left, however unlikely to prove a cure, must nevertheless do so. Hence the fanaticism of Marxists, Freudians, Eugenists, Spiritualists, Douglasites, Federal Unionists, Vegetarians, and all the rest. But I have received no assurance that anything we can do will eradicate suffering. I think the best results are obtained by people who work quietly away at their objectives, such as the abolition of the slave trade, or prison reform, or factory acts, or tuberculosis, not by those who think they can achieve universal justice, or health, or peace. I think the art of life consists in tackling each immediate evil as well as we can. To avert or postpone one particular war by wise policy, or to render one particular campaign shorter by strength and skill or less terrible by mercy to the conquered and the civilians, is more useful than all the proposals for universal peace that have ever been made; just as the dentist who can stop one toothache has deserved better of humanity than all the men who think they have some scheme for producing a perfectly healthy race.

I do not therefore find any very clear and cogent reason for inferring from the general principle of beneficence the conclusion that I must disobey if I am called on by lawful authority to be a soldier. I turn next to consider Authority. Authority is either special or general, and again either human or divine.

The special human authority which rests on me in this matter is that of the society to which I belong. That society by its declaration of war has decided the issue against Pacifism in this particular instance, and by its institutions and practice for centuries has decided against Pacifism in general. If I am a Pacifist, I have Arthur and Aelfred, Elizabeth and Cromwell, Walpole and Burke, against me. I have my university, my school, and my parents against me. I have the literature of my country against me, and cannot even open my *Beowulf,* my Shakespeare, my Johnson or my Wordsworth without being reproved. Now, of course, this authority of England is not final. But there is a difference between conclusive authority and authority of no weight at all. Men may differ as to the weight they would give the almost unanimous authority of England. I am not here concerned with assessing it but merely with noting that whatever weight it has is against Pacifism. And, of course, my duty to take that authority into account is increased by the fact that I am indebted to that society for my birth and my upbringing, for the education which has allowed me to become a Pacifist, and the tolerant laws which allow me to remain one.

Compelling Reason

So much for special human authority. The sentence of general human authority is equally clear. From the dawn of history down to the sinking of the *Terris Bay*, the world echoes with the praise of righteous war. To be a Pacifist, I must part company with Homer and Virgil, with Plato and Aristotle, with Zarathustra and the *Bhagavad-Gita*, with Cicero and Montaigne, with Iceland and with Egypt. From this point of view, I am almost tempted to reply to the Pacifist as Johnson replied to Goldsmith, 'Nay Sir, if you will not take the universal opinion of mankind, I have no more to say.'

I am aware that, though Hooker thought 'the general and perpetual voice of men is as the sentence of God Himself', yet many who hear will give it little or no weight. This disregard of human authority may have two roots. It may spring from the belief that human history is a simple, unilinear movement from worse to better – what is called a belief in Progress – so that any given generation is always in all respects wiser than all previous generations. To those who believe thus, our ancestors are superseded and there seems nothing improbable in the claim that the whole world was wrong until the day before yesterday and now has suddenly become right. With such people I confess I cannot argue, for I do not share their basic assumption. Believers in progress rightly note that in the world of machines the new model supersedes the old; from this they falsely infer a similar kind of supercession in such things as virtue and wisdom.

But human authority may be discounted on a quite different ground. It may be held, at least by a Christian Pacifist, that the human race is fallen and corrupt, so that even the consent of great and wise human teachers and great nations widely separated in time and place affords no clue whatsoever to the good. If this contention is being made, we must then turn to our next head, that of Divine Authority.

I shall consider Divine Authority only in terms of Christianity.

Of the other civilized religions I believe that only one – Buddhism – is genuinely Pacifist; and anyway I am not well enough informed about them to discuss them with profit. And when we turn to Christianity, we find Pacifism based almost exclusively on certain of the sayings of Our Lord Himself. If those sayings do not establish the Pacifist position, it is vain to try to base it on the general *securus judicat* of Christendom as a whole. For when I seek guidance there, I find Authority on the whole against me. Looking at the statement which is my immediate authority as an Anglican, the Thirty-Nine Articles, I find it laid down in black and white that 'it is lawful for Christian men, at the commandment of the Magistrate, to wear weapons and serve in the wars'. Dissenters may not accept this; then I can refer them to the history of the Presbyterians, which is by no means Pacifist. Papists may not accept this; then I can refer them to the ruling of Thomas Aquinas that 'even as princes lawfully defend their land by the sword against disturbance from within, so it belongs to them to defend it by the sword from enemies without.' Or if you demand patristic authority, I give you St Augustine, 'If Christian discipleship wholly reprobated war, then to those who sought the counsel of salvation in the Gospel this answer would have been given first, that they should throw away their arms and withdraw themselves altogether from being soldiers. But what was really said to them was, "Do violence to no man and be content with your pay". When he bade them to be content with their due soldiers' pay, he forbade them not to be paid as soldiers.' But of checking individual voices, there would be no end. All bodies that claim to be Churches – that is, who claim apostolic succession and accept the Creeds – have constantly blessed what they regarded as righteous arms. Doctors, bishops and popes – including, I think, the present Pope [Pius XII] – have again and again discountenanced the Pacifist position. Nor, I think, do we find a word about Pacifism in the apostolic writings, which are older than the gospels and represent, if anything does, that original Christendom whereof the gospels themselves are a product.

The whole Christian case for Pacifism rests, therefore, on certain Dominical utterances, such as 'Resist not evil: but whosoever shall smite thee on thy right cheek, turn to him the other also.' I am now to deal with the Christian who says this is to be taken without qualification. I need not point out – for it has doubtless been pointed out to you before – that such a Christian is obliged to take all the other hard sayings of Our Lord in the same way. For the man who has done so, who has on every occasion given to all who ask him and has finally given all he has to the poor, no one will fail to feel respect. With such a man I must suppose myself to be arguing; for who would deem worth answering that inconsistent person who takes Our Lord's words *à la rigueur* when they dispense him from a possible obligation, and takes them with latitude when they demand that he should become a pauper?

There are three ways of taking the command to turn the other cheek. One is the Pacifist interpretation; it means what it says and imposes a duty of non-resistance on all men in all circumstances. Another is the minimizing interpretation; it does not mean what it says but is merely an orientally hyperbolical way of saying that you should put up with a lot and be placable. Both you and I agree in rejecting this view. The conflict is therefore between the Pacifist interpretation and a third one which I am now going to propound. I think the text means exactly what it says, but with an understood reservation in favour of those obviously exceptional cases which every hearer would naturally assume to be exceptions without being told. Or to put the same thing in more logical language, I think the duty of non-resistance is here stated as regards injuries *simpliciter*, but without prejudice to anything we may have to allow later about injuries *secundum quid.* That is, in so far as the only relevant factors in the case are an injury to me by my neighbour and a desire on my part to retaliate, then I hold that Christianity commands the absolute mortification of that desire. No quarter whatever is given to the voice within us which says, 'He's done it to me, so I'll do the same to him'. But the moment you introduce other factors, of course, the problem is altered. Does anyone suppose that Our Lord's hearers understood Him to mean that if a homicidal maniac, attempting to murder a third party, tried to knock me out of the way, I must stand aside and let him get his victim? I at any rate think it impossible they could have so understood Him. I think it equally impossible that they supposed Him to mean that the best way of bringing up a child was to let it hit its parents whenever it was in a temper, or, when it had grabbed at the jam, to give it the honey also. I think the meaning of the words was perfectly clear – 'In so far as you are simply an angry man who has been hurt, mortify your anger and do not hit back' – even, one would have assumed that in so far as you are a magistrate struck by a private person, a parent struck by a child, a teacher by a scholar, a sane man by a lunatic, or a soldier by the public enemy, your duties may be very different, different because they may be then other motives than egoistic retaliation for hitting back. Indeed, as the audience were private people in a disarmed nation, it seems unlikely that they would have ever supposed Our Lord to be referring to war. War was not what they would have been thinking of. The frictions of daily life among villagers were more likely to be in their minds.

That is my chief reason for preferring this interpretation to yours. Any saying is to be taken in the sense it would naturally have borne in the time and place of utterance. But I also think that, so taken, it harmonizes better with St John Baptist's words to the soldiers, and with the fact that one of the few persons whom Our Lord praised without reservation was a Roman centurion. It also allows me to suppose that the New Testament is consistent with itself. St Paul approves of the magistrate's use of the sword (Romans 13:4) and so does St Peter (1 Peter 2:14). If Our Lord's words are taken in the unqualified sense which the Pacifist demands, we shall then be forced to the conclusion that Christ's true meaning, concealed from those who lived in the same time and spoke the same language, and whom He Himself chose to be His messengers to the world, as well as from all their successors, has at last been discovered in our own time. I know there are people who will not find this sort of thing difficult to believe, just as there are people ready to maintain that the true meaning of Plato or Shakespeare, oddly concealed from their contemporaries and immediate successors, has preserved its virginity for the daring embraces of one or two modern professors. But I cannot apply to divine matters a method of exegesis which I have already rejected with contempt in my profane studies. Any theory which bases itself on a supposed 'historical Jesus', to be dug out of the gospels and then set up in opposition to Christian teaching, is suspect. There have been too many historical Jesuses – a liberal Jesus, a pneumatic Jesus, a Barthian Jesus, a Marxist Jesus. They are the cheap crop of each publisher's list, like the new Napoleons and new Queen Victorias. It is not to such phantoms that I look for my faith and my salvation.

Christian authority, then, fails me in my search for Pacifism. It remains to inquire whether, if I still remain a Pacifist, I ought to suspect the secret influence of any passion. I hope you will not here misunderstand me. I do not intend to join in any of the jibes to which those of your persuasion are exposed in the popular press. Let me say at the outset that I think it unlikely there is anyone present less courageous than myself. But let me also say that there is no man alive so virtuous that he need feel himself insulted at being asked to consider the possibility of a warping passion when the choice is one between so much happiness and so much misery. For let us make no mistake. All that we fear from all the kinds of adversity, severally, is collected together in the life of a soldier on active service. Like sickness, it threatens pain and death. Like poverty, it threatens ill lodging, cold, heat, thirst and hunger. Like slavery, it threatens toil, humiliation, injustice and arbitrary rule. Like exile, it separates you from all you love. Like the galleys, it imprisons you at close quarters with uncongenial companions. It threatens *every* temporal evil – every evil except dishonour and final perdition, and those who bear it like it no better than you would like it. On the other side, though it may not be your fault, it is certainly a fact that Pacifism threatens you with almost nothing. Some public opprobrium, yes, from people whose opinion you discount and whose society you do not frequent, soon recompensed by the warm mutual approval which exists, inevitably, in any minority group. For the rest it offers you a continuance of the life you know and love, among the people and in the surroundings you know and love. It offers you time to lay the foundations of a career; for whether you will or no, you can hardly help getting the jobs for which the discharged soldiers will one day look in vain. You do not even have to fear, as Pacifists may have had to fear in the last war, that public opinion will punish you when the peace comes. For we have learned now that though the world is slow to forgive, it is quick to forget.

This, then, is why I am not a Pacifist. If I tried to become one, I should find a very doubtful factual basis, an obscure train of reasoning, a weight of authority both human and Divine against me, and strong grounds for suspecting that my wishes had directed my decision. As I have said, moral decisions do not admit of mathematical certainty. It may be, after all, that Pacifism is right. But it seems to me very long odds, longer odds than I would care to take with the voice of almost all humanity against me.

2 Bulverism

or, *The Foundation of Twentieth-century Thought*
(1941)

It is a disastrous discovery, as Emerson says somewhere, that we exist. I mean, it is disastrous when instead of merely attending to a rose we are forced to think of ourselves looking at the rose, with a certain type of mind and a certain type of eyes. It is disastrous because, if you are not very careful, the colour of the rose gets attributed to our optic nerves and its scent to our noses, and in the end there is no rose left. The professional philosophers have been bothered about this universal black-out for over two hundred years, and the world has not much listened to them. But the same disaster is now occurring on a level we can all understand.

We have recently 'discovered that we exist' in two new senses. The Freudians have discovered that we exist as bundles of complexes. The Marxians have discovered that we exist as members of some economic class. In the old days it was supposed that if a thing seemed obviously true to a hundred men, then it was probably true in fact. Nowadays the Freudian will tell you to go and analyse the hundred: you will find that they all think Elizabeth [I] a great queen because they all have a mother-complex. Their thoughts are psychologically tainted at the source. And the Marxist will tell you to go and examine the economic interests of the hundred; you will find that they all think freedom a good thing because they are all members of the bourgeoisie whose prosperity is increased by a policy of *laissez-faire*. Their thoughts are 'ideologically tainted' at the source.

Now this is obviously great fun; but it has not always been noticed that there is a bill to pay for it. There are two questions that people who say this kind of thing ought to be asked. The first is, Are *all* thoughts thus tainted at the source, or only some? The second is, Does the taint invalidate the tainted thought – in the sense of making it untrue – or not?

If they say that *all* thoughts are thus tainted, then, of course, we must remind them that Freudianism and Marxism are as much systems of thought as Christian theology or philosophical idealism. The Freudian and the Marxian are in the same boat with all the rest of us, and cannot criticize us from outside. They have sawn off the branch they were sitting on. If, on the other hand, they say that the taint need not invalidate their thinking, then neither need it invalidate ours. In which case they have saved their own branch, but also saved ours along with it.

The only line they can really take is to say that some thoughts are tainted and others are not – which has the advantage (if Freudians and Marxians regard it as an advantage) of being what every sane man has always believed. But if that is so, we must then ask how you find out which are tainted and which are not. It is no earthly use saying that those are tainted which agree with the secret wishes of the thinker. *Some* of the things I should like to believe must in fact be true; it is impossible to arrange a universe which contradicts everyone's wishes, in every respect, at every moment. Suppose I think, after doing my accounts, that I have a large balance at the bank. And suppose you want to find out whether this belief of mine is 'wishful thinking'. You can never come to any conclusion by examining my psychological condition. Your only chance of finding out is to sit down and work through the sum yourself. When you have checked my figures, then, and then only will you know whether I have that balance or not. If you find my arithmetic correct, then no amount of vapouring about my psychological condition can be anything but a waste of time. If you find my arithmetic wrong, then it may be relevant to explain psychologically how I came to be so bad at my arithmetic, and the doctrine of the concealed wish will become relevant – but only *after* you have yourself done the sum and discovered me to be wrong on purely arithmetical grounds. It is the same with all thinking and all systems of thought. If you try to find out which are tainted by speculating about the wishes of the thinkers, you are merely making a fool of yourself. You must find out on purely logical grounds which of them do, in fact, break down as arguments. Afterwards, if you like, go on and discover the psychological causes of the error.

In other words, you must show *that* a man is wrong before you start explaining *why* he is wrong. The modern method is to assume without discussion *that* he is wrong and then distract his attention from this (the only real issue) by busily explaining how he became so silly. In the course of the last fifteen years I have found this vice so common that I have had to invent a name for it. I call it Bulverism. Some day I am going to write the biography of its imaginary inventor, Ezekiel Bulver, whose destiny was determined at the age of five when he heard his mother say to his father – who had been maintaining that two sides of a triangle were together greater than the third – 'Oh, you say that *because you are a man.*' 'At that moment', E. Bulver assures us, 'there flashed across my opening mind the great truth that refutation is no necessary part of argument. Assume that your opponent is wrong, and then explain his error, and the world will be at your feet. Attempt to prove that he is wrong or (worse still) try to find out whether he is wrong or right, and the national dynamism of our age will thrust you to the wall.' That is how Bulver became one of the makers of the Twentieth Century.

I find the fruits of his discovery almost everywhere. Thus I see my religion dismissed on the grounds that 'the comfortable parson had every reason for assuring the nineteenth-century worker that poverty would be rewarded in another world'. Well, no doubt he had. On the assumption that Christianity is an error, I can see easily enough that some people would still have a motive for inculcating it. I see it so easily that I can, of course, play the game the other way round, by saying that 'the modern man has every reason for trying to convince himself that there are no eternal sanctions behind the morality he is rejecting'. For Bulverism is a truly democratic game in the sense that all can play it all day long, and that it gives no unfair privilege to the small and offensive minority who reason. But of course it gets us not one inch nearer to deciding whether, as a matter of fact, the Christian religion is true or false. That question remains to be discussed on quite different grounds – a matter of philosophical and historical argument. However it were decided, the improper motives of some people, both for believing it and for disbelieving it, would remain just as they are.

I see Bulverism at work in every political argument. The capitalists must be bad economists because we know why they want capitalism, and equally the Communists must be bad economists because we know why they want Communism. Thus, the Bulverists on both sides. In reality, of course, either the doctrines of the capitalists are false, or the doctrines of the Communists, or both; but you can only find out the rights and wrongs by reasoning – never by being rude about your opponent's psychology.

Until Bulverism is crushed, reason can play no effective part in human affairs. Each side snatches it early as a weapon against the other; but between the two reason itself is discredited. And why should reason not be discredited? It would be easy, in answer, to point to the present state of the world, but the real answer is even more immediate. The forces discrediting reason, themselves depend on reasoning. You must reason even to Bulverize. You are trying to *prove* that all *proofs* are invalid. If you fail, you fail. If you succeed, then you fail even more – for the proof that all proofs are invalid must be invalid itself.

The alternative then is either sheer self-contradicting idiocy or else some tenacious belief in our power of reasoning, held in the teeth of all the evidence that Bulverists can bring for a 'taint' in this or that human reasoner. I am ready to admit, if you like, that this tenacious belief has something transcendental or mystical about it. What then? Would you rather be a lunatic than a mystic?

So we see there is justification for holding on to our belief in Reason. But can this be done without theism? Does 'I know' involve that God exists? Everything I know is an inference from sensation (except the present moment). All our knowledge of the universe beyond our immediate experiences depends on inferences from these experiences. If our inferences do not give a genuine insight into reality, then we can know nothing. A theory cannot be accepted if it does not allow our thinking to be a genuine insight, nor if the fact of our knowledge is not explicable in terms of that theory.

But our thoughts can only be accepted as a genuine insight under certain conditions. All beliefs have causes but a distinction must be drawn between (1) ordinary causes and (2) a special kind of cause called 'a reason'. Causes are mindless events which can produce other results than belief. Reasons arise from axioms and inferences and affect only beliefs. Bulverism tries to show that the other man has causes and not reasons and that we have reasons and not causes. A belief which can be accounted for entirely in terms of causes is worthless. This principle must not be abandoned when we consider the beliefs which are the basis of others. Our knowledge depends on our certainty about axioms and inferences. If these are the result of causes, then there is no possibility of knowledge. Either we can know nothing *or* thought has reasons only, and no causes.

3 First and Second Things (1942)

When I read in *Time and Tide* on 6th June [1942] that the Germans have selected Hagen in preference to Siegfried as their national hero, I could have laughed out loud for pleasure. For I am a romantic person who has frankly revelled in my Nibelungs, and specially in Wagner's version of the story, ever since one golden summer in adolescence when I first heard the 'Ride of the Valkyries' on a gramophone and saw Arthur Rackham's illustrations to *The Ring*. Even now the very smell of those volumes can come over me with the poignancy of remembered calf-love. It was, therefore, a bitter moment when the Nazis took over my treasure and made it part of their ideology. But now all is well. They have proved unable to digest it. They can retain it only by standing the story on its head and making one of the minor villains the hero. Doubtless the logic of their position will presently drive them further, and Alberich will be announced as the true personification of the Nordic spirit. In the meantime, they have given me back what they stole.

The mention of the Nordic spirit reminds me that their attempted appropriation of *The Ring* is only one instance of their larger attempt to appropriate 'the Nordic' as a whole, and this larger attempt is equally ridiculous. What business have people who call might right to say they are worshippers of Odin? The whole point about Odin was that he had the right but not the might. The whole point about Norse religion was that it alone of all mythologies told men to serve gods who were admittedly fighting with their backs to the wall and would certainly be

23

defeated in the end. 'I am off to die with Odin' said the rover in Stevenson's fable,[1] thus proving that Stevenson understood something about the Nordic spirit which Germany has never been able to understand at all. The gods will fall. The wisdom of Odin, the humorous courage of Thor (Thor was something of a Yorkshireman) and the beauty of Balder will all be smashed eventually by the *Realpolitik* of the stupid giants and misshapen trolls. But that does not in the least alter the allegiance of any free man. Hence, as we should expect, real Germanic poetry is all about heroic stands, and fighting against hopeless odds.

At this stage it occurred to me that I had stumbled on a rather remarkable paradox. How is it that the only people in Europe who have tried to revive their pre-Christian mythology as a living faith should also be the people that shows itself incapable of understanding that mythology in its very rudiments? The retrogression would, in any case, be deplorable – just as it would be deplorable if a full grown man reverted to the *ethos* of his preparatory school. But you would expect him at least to get the no-sneaking rule right, and to be quite clear that new boys ought not to put their hands in their pockets. To sacrifice the greater good for the less and then not to get the lesser good after all – that is the surprising folly. To sell one's birthright for a mess of mythology and then to get the mythology all wrong – how did they do it? For it is quite clear that I (who would rather paint my face bright blue with woad than suggest that there is a real Odin) am actually getting out of Odin all the good and all the fun that Odin can supply, while the Nazi Odinists are getting none of it.

And yet, it seemed to me as I thought about it, this may not be such a paradox as it looks. Or, at least, it is a paradox which turns

---

[1] This is found in R. L. Stevenson's 'Faith, Half-Faith, and No Faith', first published in *The Strange Case of Dr Jekyll and Mr Hyde with other Fables* (London, 1896).

up so often that a man ought by now to be accustomed to it. Other instances began to come to mind. Until quite modern times – I think, until the time of the Romantics – nobody ever suggested that literature and the arts were an end in themselves. They 'belonged to the ornamental part of life', they provided 'innocent diversion'; or else they 'refined our manners' or 'incited us to virtue' or glorified the gods. The great music had been written for Masses, the great pictures painted to fill up a space on the wall of a noble patron's dining-room or to kindle devotion in a church; the great tragedies were produced either by religious poets in honour of Dionysus or by commercial poets to entertain Londoners on half-holidays. It was only in the nineteenth century that we became aware of the full dignity of art. We began to 'take it seriously' as the Nazis take mythology seriously. But the result seems to have been a dislocation of the aesthetic life in which little is left us but high-minded works which fewer and fewer people want to read or hear or see, and 'popular' works of which both those who make them and those who enjoy them are half ashamed. Just like the Nazis, by valuing too highly a real, but subordinate good, we have come near to losing that good itself.

The longer I looked into it the more I came to suspect that I was perceiving a universal law. *On cause mieux quand on ne dit pas Causons.*[1] The woman who makes a dog the centre of her life loses, in the end, not only her human usefulness and dignity but even the proper pleasure of dog-keeping. The man who makes alcohol his chief good loses not only his job but his palate and all power of enjoying the earlier (and only pleasurable) levels of intoxication. It is a glorious thing to feel for a moment or two that the whole meaning of the universe is summed up in one woman – glorious so long as other duties and pleasures keep

[1] One converses better when one does not say 'Let us converse'.

tearing you away from her. But clear the decks and so arrange your life (it is sometimes feasible) that you will have nothing to do but contemplate her, and what happens? Of course this law has been discovered before, but it will stand re-discovery. It may be stated as follows: every preference of a small good to a great, or a partial good to a total good, involves the loss of the small or partial good for which the sacrifice was made.

Apparently the world is made that way. If Esau really got the pottage in return for his birthright,[1] then Esau was a lucky exception. You can't get second things by putting them first; you can get second things only by putting first things first. From which it would follow that the question, 'What things are first?', is of concern not only to philosophers but to everyone.

It is impossible, in this context, not to inquire what our own civilization has been putting first for the last thirty years. And the answer is plain. It has been putting itself first. To preserve civilization has been the great aim; the collapse of civilization, the great bugbear. Peace, a high standard of life, hygiene, transport, science and amusement – all these, which are what we usually mean by civilization, have been our ends. It will be replied that our concern for civilization is very natural and very necessary at a time when civilization is so imperilled. But how if the shoe is on the other foot? – how if civilization has been imperilled precisely by the fact that we have all made civilization our *summum bonum?* Perhaps it can't be preserved in that way. Perhaps civilization will never be safe until we care for something else more than we care for it.

The hypothesis has certain facts to support it. As far as peace (which is one ingredient in our idea of civilization) is concerned, I think many would now agree that a foreign policy dominated by desire for peace is one of the many roads that lead to war. And

[1] Genesis 25.

26

was civilization ever seriously endangered until civilization became the exclusive aim of human activity? There is much rash idealization of past ages about, and I do not wish to encourage more of it. Our ancestors were cruel, lecherous, greedy and stupid, like ourselves. But while they cared for other things more than for civilization – and they cared at different times for all sorts of things, for the will of God, for glory, for personal honour, for doctrinal purity, for justice – was civilization often in serious danger of disappearing?

At least the suggestion is worth a thought. To be sure, if it were true that civilization will never be safe till it is put second, that immediately raises the question, second to what? What is the first thing? The only reply I can offer here is that if we do not know, then the first, and only truly practical thing, is to set about finding out.

4 Equality (1943)

I am a democrat because I believe in the Fall of Man. I think
most people are democrats for the opposite reason. A great deal
of democratic enthusiasm descends from the ideas of people like
Rousseau, who believed in democracy because they thought
mankind so wise and good that everyone deserved a share in the
government. The danger of defending democracy on those
grounds is that they're not true. And whenever their weakness is
exposed, the people who prefer tyranny make capital out of the
exposure. I find that they're not true without looking further
than myself. I don't deserve a share in governing a hen-roost,
much less a nation. Nor do most people – all the people who
believe advertisements, and think in catchwords and spread
rumours. The real reason for democracy is just the reverse.
Mankind is so fallen that no man can be trusted with unchecked
power over his fellows. Aristotle said that some people were only
fit to be slaves. I do not contradict him. But I reject slavery
because I see no men fit to be masters.

This introduces a view of equality rather different from that in
which we have been trained. I do not think that equality is one of
those things (like wisdom or happiness) which are good simply
in themselves and for their own sakes. I think it is in the same
class as medicine, which is good because we are ill, or clothes
which are good because we are no longer innocent. I don't think
the old authority in kings, priests, husbands, or fathers, and the
old obedience in subjects, laymen, wives, and sons, was in itself a
degrading or evil thing at all. I think it was intrinsically as good

and beautiful as the nakedness of Adam and Eve. It was rightly taken away because men became bad and abused it. To attempt to restore it now would be the same error as that of the Nudists. Legal and economic equality are absolutely necessary remedies for the Fall, and protection against cruelty.

But medicine is not good. There is no spiritual sustenance in flat equality. It is a dim recognition of this fact which makes much of our political propaganda sound so thin. We are trying to be enraptured by something which is merely the negative condition of the good life. And that is why the imagination of people is so easily captured by appeals to the craving for inequality, whether in a romantic form of films about loyal courtiers or in the brutal form of Nazi ideology. The tempter always works on some *real* weakness in our own system of values: offers food to some need which we have starved.

When equality is treated not as a medicine or a safety-gadget but as an ideal we begin to breed that stunted and envious sort of mind which hates all superiority. That mind is the special disease of democracy, as cruelty and servility are the special diseases of privileged societies. It will kill us all if it grows unchecked. The man who cannot conceive a joyful and loyal obedience on the one hand, nor an unembarrassed and noble acceptance of that obedience on the other, the man who has never even wanted to kneel or to bow, is a prosaic barbarian. But it would be wicked folly to restore these old inequalities on the legal or external plane. Their proper place is elsewhere.

We must wear clothes since the Fall. Yes, but inside, under what Milton called 'these troublesome disguises',[1] we want the naked body, that is, the *real* body, to be alive. We want it, on proper occasions, to appear: in the marriage-chamber, in the public privacy of a men's bathing-place, and (of course) when

[1] John Milton, *Paradise Lost* (1667), Book IV, line 740.

any medical or other emergency demands. In the same way, under the necessary outer covering of legal equality, the whole hierarchical dance and harmony of our deep and joyously accepted spiritual inequalities should be alive. It is there, of course, in our life as Christians: there, as laymen, we can obey – all the more because the priest has no authority over us on the political level. It is there in our relation to parents and teachers – all the more because it is now a willed and wholly spiritual reverence. It should be there also in marriage.

This last point needs a little plain speaking. Men have so horribly abused their power over women in the past that to wives, of all people, equality is in danger of appearing as an ideal. But Mrs Naomi Mitchison has laid her finger on the real point. Have as much equality as you please – the more the better – in our marriage laws: but at some level consent to inequality, nay, delight in inequality, is an *erotic* necessity. Mrs Mitchison speaks of women so fostered on a defiant idea of equality that the mere sensation of the male embrace rouses an undercurrent of resentment. Marriages are thus shipwrecked.[1] This is the tragi-comedy of the modern woman; taught by Freud to consider the act of love the most important thing in life, and then inhibited by feminism from that internal surrender which alone can make it a complete emotional success. Merely for the sake of her own erotic pleasure, to go no further, some degree of obedience and humility seems to be (normally) necessary on the woman's part.

The error here has been to assimilate all forms of affection to that special form we call friendship. It indeed does imply equality. But it is quite different from the various loves within the same household. Friends are not primarily absorbed in each other. It is when we are doing things together that friendship springs up –

---

[1] Naomi Mitchison, *The Home and a Changing Civilisation* (London, 1934), Chapter 1, pp. 49–50.

painting, sailing ships, praying, philosophizing, fighting shoulder to shoulder. Friends look in the same direction. Lovers look at each other: that is, in opposite directions. To transfer bodily all that belongs to one relationship into the other is blundering.

We Britons should rejoice that we have contrived to reach much legal democracy (we still need more of the economic) without losing our ceremonial Monarchy. For there, right in the midst of our lives, is that which satisfies the craving for inequality, and acts as a permanent reminder that medicine is not food. Hence a man's reaction to Monarchy is a kind of test. Monarchy can easily be 'debunked'; but watch the faces, mark well the accents, of the debunkers. These are the men whose tap-root in Eden has been cut: whom no rumour of the polyphony, the dance, can reach – men to whom pebbles laid in a row are more beautiful than an arch. Yet even if they desire mere equality they cannot reach it. Where men are forbidden to honour a king they honour millionaires, athletes, or film-stars instead: even famous prostitutes or gangsters. For spiritual nature, like bodily nature, will be served; deny it food and it will gobble poison.

And that is why this whole question is of practical importance. Every intrusion of the spirit that says 'I'm as good as you' into our personal and spiritual life is to be resisted just as jealously as every intrusion of bureaucracy or privilege into our politics. Hierarchy within can alone preserve egalitarianism without. Romantic attacks on democracy will come again. We shall never be safe unless we already understand in our hearts all that the anti-democrats can say, and have provided for it better than they. Human nature will not permanently endure flat equality if it is extended from its proper political field into the more real, more concrete fields within. Let us *wear* equality; but let us undress every night.

5 Three Kinds of Men (1943)

There are three kinds of people in the world. The first class is of those who live simply for their own sake and pleasure, regarding Man and Nature as so much raw material to be cut up into whatever shape may serve them. In the second class are those who acknowledge some other claim upon them – the will of God, the categorical imperative, or the good of society – and honestly try to pursue their own interests no further than this claim will allow. They try to surrender to the higher claim as much as it demands, like men paying a tax, but hope, like other taxpayers, that what is left over will be enough for them to live on. Their life is divided, like a soldier's or a schoolboy's life, into time 'on parade' and 'off parade', 'in school' and 'out of school'. But the third class is of those who can say like St Paul that for them 'to live is Christ'.[1] These people have got rid of the tiresome business of adjusting the rival claims of Self and God by the simple expedient of rejecting the claims of Self altogether. The old egoistic will has been turned round, reconditioned, and made into a new thing. The will of Christ no longer limits theirs; it is theirs. All their time, in belonging to Him, belongs also to them, for they are His.

And because there are three classes, any merely twofold division of the world into good and bad is disastrous. It overlooks the fact that the members of the second class (to which most of us belong) are always and necessarily unhappy. The tax which

---

[1] Philippians 1:21.

moral conscience levies on our desires does not in fact leave us enough to live on. As long as we are in this class we must either feel guilt because we have not paid the tax or penury because we have. The Christian doctrine that there is no 'salvation' by works done according to the moral law is a fact of daily experience. Back or on we must go. But there is no going on simply by our own efforts. If the new Self, the new Will, does not come at His own good pleasure to be born in us, we cannot produce Him synthetically.

The price of Christ is something, in a way, much easier than moral effort – it is to want Him. It is true that the wanting itself would be beyond our power but for one fact. The world is so built that, to help us desert our own satisfactions, they desert us. War and trouble and finally old age take from us one by one all those things that the natural Self hoped for at its setting out. Begging is our only wisdom, and want in the end makes it easier for us to be beggars. Even on those terms the Mercy will receive us.

6 'Horrid Red Things' (1944)

Many theologians and some scientists are now ready to proclaim that the nineteenth-century 'conflict between science and religion' is over and done with. But even if this is true, it is a truth known only to real theologians and real scientists – that is, to a few highly educated men. To the man in the street the conflict is still perfectly real, and in his mind it takes a form which the learned hardly dream of.

The ordinary man is not thinking of particular dogmas and particular scientific discoveries. What troubles him is an all-pervading difference of atmosphere between what he believes Christianity to be and that general picture of the universe which he has picked up from living in a scientific age. He gathers from the Creed that God has a 'Son' (just as if God were a god, like Odin or Jupiter): that this Son 'came down' (like a parachutist) from 'Heaven', first to earth and later to some land of the dead situated beneath the earth's surface: that, still later, He ascended into the sky and took His seat in a decorated chair placed a little to the right of His Father's throne. The whole thing seems to imply a local and material heaven – a palace in the stratosphere – a flat earth and all the rest of those archaic misconceptions.

The ordinary man is well aware that we should deny all the beliefs he attributes to us and interpret our Creed in a different sense. But this by no means satisfies him. 'No doubt,' he thinks, 'once those articles of belief are there, they can be allegorized or spiritualized away to any extent you please. But is it not plain that they would never have been there at all if the first generation of Christians had had any notion of what the real universe is like? A historian who has based his work on the misreading of a document, may afterwards (when his mistake had been exposed) exercise great ingenuity in showing that his account of a certain battle can still be reconciled with what the document records. But the point is that none of these ingenious explanations would ever have come into existence if he had read his documents correctly at the outset. They are therefore really a waste of labour; it would be manlier of him to admit his mistake and begin over again.'

I think there are two things that Christians must do if they wish to convince this 'ordinary' modern man. In the first place, they must make it quite clear that what will remain of the Creed after all their explanations and reinterpretations will still be something quite unambiguously supernatural, miraculous, and shocking. We may not believe in a flat earth and a sky-palace. But we must insist from the beginning that we believe, as firmly as any savage or theosophist, in a spirit-world which can, and does, invade the natural or phenomenal universe. For the plain man suspects that when we start explaining, we are going to explain away: that we have mythology for our ignorant hearers and are ready, when cornered by educated hearers, to reduce it to innocuous moral platitudes which no one ever dreamed of denying. And there are theologians who justify this suspicion. From them we must part company absolutely. If nothing remains except what could be equally well stated without Christian formulae, then the honest thing is to admit that Christianity is untrue and to begin over again without it.

In the second place, we must try to teach something about the difference between thinking and imagining. It is, of course, a historical error to suppose that all, or even most, early Christians believed in the sky-palace in the same sense in which we believe in the solar system. Anthropomorphism was condemned by the Church as soon as the question was explicitly before her. But some early Christians may have done this; and probably thousands never thought of their faith without anthropomorphic imagery. That is why we must distinguish the core of belief from the attendant imagining.

When I think of London I always see a picture of Euston Station. But I do not believe that London *is* Euston Station. That is a simple case, because there the thinker *knows* the imagery to be false. Now let us take a more complex one. I once heard a lady tell her daughter that if you ate too many aspirin tablets you would die. 'But why?' asked the child. 'If you squash them you don't find any horrid red things inside them.' Obviously, when this child thought of poison she not only had an attendant image of 'horrid red things', but she actually believed that poison was red. And this is an error. But how far does it invalidate her thinking about poison? She learned that an overdose of aspirin would kill you; her belief was true. She knew, within limits, which of the substances in her mother's house were poisonous. If I, staying in the house, had raised a glass of what looked like water to my lips, and the child had said, 'Don't drink that. Mummie says it's poisonous,' I should have been foolish to disregard the warning on the ground that 'This child has an archaic and mythological idea of poison as horrid red things.'

There is thus a distinction not only between thought and imagination in general, but even between thought and those images which the thinker (falsely) believes to be true. When the child learned later that poison is not always red, she would not have felt that anything essential in her beliefs about poison had been altered. She would still know, as she had always known, that poison is what kills you if you swallow it. That is the essence of poison. The erroneous beliefs about colour drop away without affecting it.

In the same way an early peasant Christian might have thought that Christ's sitting at the right hand of the Father really implied two chairs of state, in a certain spatial relation, inside a sky-palace. But if the same man afterwards received a philosophical education and discovered that God has no body, parts, or passions, and therefore neither a right hand nor a palace, he would not have felt that the essentials of his belief had been altered. What had mattered to him, even in the days of his simplicity, had not been supposed details about celestial furniture. It had been the assurance that the once crucified Master was now the supreme Agent of the unimaginable Power on whom the whole universe depends. And he would recognize that in this he had never been deceived.

The critic may still ask us why the imagery – which we admit to be untrue - should be used at all. But he has not noticed that any language we attempt to substitute for it would involve imagery that is open to all the same objections. To say that God 'enters' the natural order involves just as much spatial imagery as to say that He 'comes down'; one has simply substituted horizontal (or undefined) for vertical movement. To say that He is 're-absorbed' into the Noumenal is better than to say He 'ascended' into Heaven, only if the picture of something dissolving in warm fluid, or being sucked into a throat, is less misleading than the picture of a bird, or a balloon, going up. All language, except about objects of sense, is metaphorical through and through. To call God a 'Force' (that is, something like a wind or a dynamo) is as metaphorical as to call Him a Father or a King. On such matters we can make our language more polysyllabic and duller: we cannot make it more literal. The difficulty is not peculiar to theologians. Scientists, poets, psychoanalysts, and metaphysicians are all in the same boat:

Man's reason is in such deep insolvency to sense.[1]

---

[1] Robert Bridges, *The Testament of Beauty*, Book I, line 57.

Where, then, do we draw the line between explaining and 'explaining away'? I do not think there is much difficulty. All that concerns the un-incarnate activities of God – His operation on that plane of being where sense cannot enter – must be taken along with imagery which we know to be, in the literal sense, untrue. But there can be no defence for applying the same treatment to the miracles of the Incarnate God. They are recorded as events on this earth which affected human senses. They are the sort of thing we can describe literally. If Christ turned water into wine, and we had been present, we could have seen, smelled, and tasted. The story that He did so is not of the same order as His 'sitting at the right hand of the Father'. It is either fact, or legend, or lie. You must take it or leave it.

7 Democratic Education (1944)

Democratic education, says Aristotle, ought to mean, not the education which democrats like, but the education which will preserve democracy. Until we have realized that the two things do not necessarily go together we cannot think clearly about education.

For example, an education which gave the able and diligent boys no advantage over the stupid and idle ones, would be in one sense democratic. It would be egalitarian and democrats like equality. The caucus-race in *Alice,* where all the competitors won and all got prizes, was a 'democratic' race: like the Garter it tolerated no nonsense about merit.[1] Such total egalitarianism in education has not yet been openly recommended. But a movement in that direction begins to appear. It can be seen in the growing demand that subjects which some boys do very much better than others should not be compulsory. Yesterday it was Latin; today, as I see from a letter in one of the papers, it is Mathematics. Both these subjects give an 'unfair advantage' to boys of a certain type. To abolish that advantage is therefore in one sense democratic.

But of course there is no reason for stopping with the abolition of these two compulsions. To be consistent we must go further.

---

[1] The Order of the Garter, instituted by King Edward III in 1344, is the highest order of knighthood. Lewis had in mind the comment made by Lord Melbourne (1779–1848) about the Order: 'I like the Garter; there is no damned merit in it.'

We must also abolish *all* compulsory subjects; and we must make the curriculum so wide that 'every boy will get a chance at something'. Even the boy who can't or won't learn his alphabet can be praised and petted for *something* – handicrafts or gymnastics, moral leadership or deportment, citizenship or the care of guinea-pigs, 'hobbies' or musical appreciation – anything he likes. Then no boy, and no boy's parents, need feel inferior.

An education on those lines will be pleasing to democratic feelings. It will have repaired the inequalities of nature. But it is quite another question whether it will breed a democratic nation which can survive, or even one whose survival is desirable.

The improbability that a nation thus educated could survive need not be laboured. Obviously it can escape destruction only if its rivals and enemies are so obliging as to adopt the same system. A nation of dunces can be safe only in a world of dunces. But the question of desirability is more interesting.

The demand for equality has two sources; one of them is among the noblest, the other is the basest, of human emotions. The noble source is the desire for fair play. But the other source is the hatred of superiority. At the present moment it would be very unrealistic to overlook the importance of the latter. There is in all men a tendency (only corrigible by good training from without and persistent moral effort from within) to resent the existence of what is stronger, subtler or better than themselves. In uncorrected and brutal men this hardens into an implacable and disinterested hatred for every kind of excellence. The vocabulary of a period tells tales. There is reason to be alarmed at the immense vogue today of such words as 'high-brow', 'up-stage', 'old school tie', 'academic', 'smug', and 'complacent'. These words, as used today, are sores: one feels the poison throbbing in them.

The kind of 'democratic' education which is already looming ahead is bad because it endeavours to propitiate evil passions, to appease envy. There are two reasons for not attempting this. In the first place, you will not succeed. Envy is insatiable. The more you concede to it the more it will demand. No attitude of humility which you can possibly adopt will propitiate a man with an inferiority complex. In the second place, you are trying to introduce equality where equality is fatal.

Equality (outside mathematics) is a purely social conception. It applies to man as a political and economic animal. It has no place in the world of the mind. Beauty is not democratic; she reveals herself more to the few than to the many, more to the persistent and disciplined seekers than to the careless. Virtue is not democratic; she is achieved by those who pursue her more hotly than most men. Truth is not democratic; she demands special talents and special industry in those to whom she gives her favours. Political democracy is doomed if it tries to extend its demand for equality into these higher spheres. Ethical, intellectual, or aesthetic democracy is death.

A truly democratic education – one which will preserve democracy – must be, in its own field, ruthlessly aristocratic, shamelessly 'high-brow'. In drawing up its curriculum it should always have chiefly in view the interests of the boy who wants to know and who can know. (With very few exceptions they are the same boy. The stupid boy, nearly always, is the boy who does not *want* to know.) It must, in a certain sense, subordinate the interests of the many to those of the few, and it must subordinate the school to the university. Only thus can it be a nursery of those first-class intellects without which neither a democracy nor any other State can thrive.

'And what', you ask, 'about the dull boy? What about our Tommy, who is so highly strung and doesn't like doing sums and grammar? Is he to be brutally sacrificed to other people's sons?' I answer: dear Madam, you quite misunderstand Tommy's real wishes and real interests. It is the 'aristocratic' system which will really give Tommy what he wants. If you let me have my way, Tommy will gravitate very comfortably to the bottom of the form; and there he will sit at the back of the room chewing caramels and conversing *sotto voce* with his peers, occasionally ragging and occasionally getting punished, and all the time imbibing that playfully intransigent attitude to authority which is our chief protection against England's becoming a servile State. When he grows up he will not be a Porson;[1] but the world will still have room for a great many more Tommies than Porsons. There are dozens of jobs (much better paid than the intellectual ones) in which he can be very useful and very happy. And one priceless benefit he will enjoy: he will know he's not clever. The distinction between him and the great brains will have been clear to him ever since, in the playground, he punched the heads containing those great brains. He will have a certain, half amused respect for them. He will cheerfully admit that, though he could knock spots off them on the golf links, they know and do what he cannot. He will be a pillar of democracy. He will allow just the right amount of rope to those clever ones.

But what you want to do is to take away from Tommy that whole free, private life as part of the everlasting opposition which is his whole desire. You have already robbed him of all real play by making games compulsory. Must you meddle further? When (during a Latin lesson really intended for his betters) he is contentedly whittling a piece of wood into a boat under the desk, must you come in to discover a 'talent' and pack him off to the woodcarving class, so that what hitherto was fun must become one more lesson? Do you think he will thank you? Half the charm of carving the boat lay in the fact that it involved a

---

[1] Richard Porson (1759–1808), son of the parish clerk at East Ruston, near North Walsham, showed extraordinary memory when a boy, and by the help of various protectors he was educated at Eton and Trinity College, Cambridge. In 1792 he became Regius Professor of Greek at Cambridge.

resistance to authority. Must you take that pleasure – a pleasure without which no true democracy can exist – away from him? Give him marks for his hobby, officialize it, finally fool the poor boy into the belief that what he is doing is just as clever 'in its own way' as real work? What do you think will come of it? When he gets out into the real world he is bound to discover the truth. He may be disappointed. Because you have turned this simple, wholesome creature into a coxcomb, he will resent those inferiorities which (but for you) would not have irked him at all. A mild pleasure in ragging, a determination not to be much interfered with, is a valuable brake on reckless planning and a valuable curb on the meddlesomeness of minor officials: envy, bleating 'I'm as good as you', is the hotbed of Fascism. You are going about to take away the one and foment the other. Democracy demands that little men should not take big ones too seriously; it dies when it is full of little men who think they are big themselves.

8 A Dream (1944)

I still think (with all respect to the Freudians) that it was the concourse of irritations during the day which was responsible for my dream.

The day had begun badly with a letter from L. about his married sister. L.'s sister is going to have a baby in a few months; her first, and that at an age which causes some anxiety. And according to L. the state of the law – if 'law' is still the right word for it – is that his sister can get some domestic help only if she takes a job. She may try to nurse and care for her child provided she shoulders a burden of housework which will prevent her from doing so or kill her in the doing: or alternatively, she can get some help with the housework provided she herself takes a job which forces her to neglect the child.

I sat down to write a letter to L. I pointed out to him that of course his sister's case was very bad, but what could he expect? We were in the midst of a life and death struggle. The women who might have helped his sister had all been diverted to even more necessary work. I had just got thus far when the noise outside my window became so loud that I jumped up to see what it was.

It was the W.A.A.F.[1] It was the W.A.A.F., not using typewriters, nor mops, nor buckets, nor saucepans, nor pot-brushes, but holding a ceremonial parade. They had a band. They even had a girl who had been taught to imitate the antics of a peacetime

[1] Women's Auxiliary Air Force.

44

Drum Major in the regular army. It is not, to my mind, the prettiest exercise in the world for the female body, but I must say she was doing it very well. You could see what endless pains and time had gone to her training. But at that moment my telephone rang.

It was a call from W. W. is a man who works very long hours in a most necessary profession. The scantiness of his leisure and the rarity of his enjoyments gives a certain sacrosanctity to all one's engagements with him: that is why I have had an evening with him on the first Wednesday of every month for more years than I can remember. It is a law of the Medes and Persians. He had rung up to say that he wouldn't be able to come this Wednesday. He is in the Home Guard, and his platoon were all being turned out that evening (all after their day's work) to practise – ceremonial slow marching. 'What about Friday?' I asked. No good; they were being paraded on Friday evening for compulsory attendance at a lecture on European affairs. 'At least', said I, 'I'll see you at church on Sunday evening.' Not a bit of it. His platoon – I happen to know that W. is the only Christian it contains – were being marched off to a different church, two miles away; a church to which W. has the strongest doctrinal objections. 'But look here,' I asked in my exasperation, 'what the blazes has all this tomfoolery got to do with the purposes for which you originally joined the old L.D.V.?'[1] W., however, had rung off.

The final blow fell that evening in Common Room. An influential person was present and I'm *almost* sure I heard him say, 'Of course we shall retain some kind of conscription after the war; but it won't necessarily have anything to do with the fighting services.' It was then that I stole away to bed and had my dream.

---

[1] The Local Defence Volunteers were organized in May 1940 for men between the ages of 17 and 65. Their purpose was to deal with German parachutists. The name was changed to the Home Guard in December 1940, and conscription began in 1941.

I dreamed that a number of us bought a ship and hired a crew and captain and went to sea. We called her the *State*. And a great storm arose and she began to make heavy weather of it, till at last there came a cry 'All hands to the pumps – owners and all!' We had too much sense to disobey the call and in less time than it takes to write the words we had all turned out, and allowed ourselves to be formed into squads at the pumps. Several emergency petty officers were appointed to teach us our work and keep us at it. In my dream I did not, even at the outset, greatly care for the look of some of these gentry; but at such a moment – the ship being nearly under – who could attend to a trifle like that? And we worked day and night at the pumps and very hard work we found it. And by the mercy of God we kept her afloat and kept her head on to it, till presently the weather improved.

I don't think that any of us expected the pumping squads to be dismissed there and then. We knew that the storm might not be really over and it was as well to be prepared for anything. We didn't even grumble (or not much) when we found that parades were to be no fewer. What did break our hearts were the things the petty officers now began to do to us when they had us on parade. They taught us nothing about pumping or handling a rope or indeed anything that might help to save their lives or ours. Either there was nothing more to learn or the petty officers did not know it. They began to teach us all sorts of things – the history of shipbuilding, the habits of mermaids, how to dance the hornpipe and play the penny whistle and chew tobacco. For by this time the emergency petty officers (though the real crew laughed at them) had become so very, very nautical that they couldn't open their mouths without saying 'Shiver my timbers' or 'Avast' or 'Belay'.

And then one day, in my dream, one of them let the cat out of the bag. We heard him say, 'Of course we shall keep all these compulsory squads in being for the next voyage: but they won't necessarily have anything to do with working the pumps. For, of course, shiver my timbers, we know there'll never be another storm, d'you see? But having once got hold of these lubbers we're not going to let them slip back again. Now's our chance to make this the sort of ship we want.'

But the emergency petty officers were doomed to disappointment. For the owners (that was 'us' in the dream, you understand) replied 'What? Lose our freedom and *not* get security in return? Why, it was only for security we surrendered our freedom at all.' And then someone cried, 'Land in sight'. And the owners with one accord took every one of the emergency petty officers by the scruff of his neck and the seat of his trousers and heaved the lot of them over the side. I protest that in my waking hours I would never have approved such an action. But the dreaming mind is regrettably immoral, and in the dream, when I saw all those meddling busybodies going *plop-plop* into the deep blue sea, I could do nothing but laugh.

My punishment was that the laughter woke me up.

9 Is English Doomed? (1944)

Great changes in the life of a nation often pass unnoticed. Probably few are aware that the serious study of English at English Universities is likely to become extinct. The death-warrant is not yet signed, but it has been made out. You may read it in the Norwood Report.[1] A balanced scheme of education must try to avoid two evils. On the one hand the interests of those boys who will never reach a University must not be sacrificed by a curriculum based on academic requirements. On the other, the liberty of the University must not be destroyed by allowing the requirements of schoolboys to dictate its forms of study. It is into this second trap that the writers of the Report have fallen. Its authors are convinced that what they mean by 'English' can be supplied 'by any teacher' (p. 94). 'Premature external examination' in this subject is deprecated (p. 96); and I am not clear when, if ever, the moment of 'maturity' is supposed to arrive. English scholars are not wanted as teachers. Universities are to devise 'a general honours degree involving English and ... some other subject' (p. 97); not because English studies will thus flourish, but to suit the schools.

---

[1] The title of 'The Norwood Report', so called after its chairman Sir Cyril Norwood, is *Curriculum and Examinations in Secondary Schools: Report of the Committee of the Secondary School Examinations Council Appointed by the President of the Board of Education in 1941* (1943). See also Lewis's essay 'The Parthenon and the Optative' in his *Of This and Other Worlds*, ed. Walter Hooper (1982). The American title of this book is *On Stories and Other Essays on Literature* (1982).

Is English Doomed? (1944)

No instructed person to whom I have talked doubts that these proposals, if accepted, mean the end of English as an academic discipline. A subject in which there are no external examinations will lead to no State scholarships; one in which no school teachers are required will lead to no livelihoods. The door into academic English, and the door out of it, have both been bricked up. The English Faculty in every University thus becomes a faculty without students. At some of the largest Universities, no doubt, there will still be a Professor of English, as there is a Professor of Sanskrit or of Byzantine Greek, and four or five students (in a good year) may attend his lectures. But as an important element in the intellectual life of the country the thing will be dead. We may confidently hope, indeed, that English scholarship will survive abroad, notably in America and Germany; it will not survive here.

There are some who will welcome this result. English faculties have a habit of being obtrusive. The strongly modernist and radical character of the Cambridge Tripos, and what has been called (with exaggeration) the disquietingly Christian flavour of the Oxford 'Schools', may each, in its different way, offend. Taken together, they are certainly a warning that if you want a mass-produced orthodoxy you will be ill-advised to let the young study our national literature, for it is a realm where *tout arrive*; but I do not think the Report was inspired by such considerations. If it kills English scholarship it will probably have done so inadvertently; its views are the result of honest misunderstanding. It believes that 'any teacher' in the course of teaching his own special subject can teach clear and logical English. The view would have been plausible when the oldest of those who made the Report were themselves at school. For them all teachers had been trained in the Classics. The results of that discipline on English style were not, it is true, so good as is often claimed, but it removed at least the worst barbarisms. Since then the Classics have almost been routed. Unless English, seriously studied, succeeds to their place, the English which 'any teacher' inculcates in the course of teaching something else will be at best the reflection of his favourite newspaper and at worst the technical jargon of his own subject.

The danger is lest the views of the Report should be generally approved (as they were possibly formed) under a misunderstanding of the real nature of English scholarship. Many will think it reasonable to examine children in Geography or (Heaven help us!) in Divinity, yet not in English, on the ground that Geography and Divinity were never intended to entertain, whereas Literature was. The teaching of English Literature, in fact, is conceived simply as an aid to 'appreciation'. And appreciation is, to be sure, a *sine qua non*. To have laughed at the jokes, shuddered at the tragedy, wept at the pathos – this is as necessary as to have learned grammar. But neither grammar nor appreciation is the ultimate End.

The true aim of literary studies is to lift the student out of his provincialism by making him 'the spectator', if not of all, yet of much, 'time and existence'. The student, or even the schoolboy, who has been brought by good (and therefore mutually disagreeing) teachers to meet the past where alone the past still lives, is taken out of the narrowness of his own age and class into a more public world. He is learning the true *Phaenomenologie des Geistes*; discovering what varieties there are in Man. 'History' alone will not do, for it studies the past mainly in secondary authorities. It is possible to 'do History' for years without knowing at the end what it felt like to be an Anglo-Saxon *eorl*, a cavalier, an eighteenth-century country gentleman. The gold behind the paper currency is to be found, almost exclusively, in literature. In it lies deliverance from the tyranny of generalizations and catchwords. Its students know (for example) what diverse realities – Launcelot, Baron Bradwardine,

Mulvaney[1] – hide behind the word *militarism*. If I regard the English Faculties at our Universities as the chief guardians (under modern conditions) of the Humanities, I may doubtless be misled by partiality for studies to which I owe so much; yet in a way I am well placed for judging. I have been pupil and teacher alike in *Literae Humaniores*, pupil and teacher alike in English; in the History School (I confess) teacher only. If anyone said that English was now the most liberal – and liberating – discipline of the three, I should not find it easy to contradict him.

'In this time, place, and fortune,' said Sidney's Musidorus, 'it is lawfull for us to speake gloriously' – for he spoke in the condemned cell.[2] If England, departing from the practice of Greece and Rome, is about to banish the systematic study of her own literature, is it an honest pride to remember before the blow falls what fruits that study has borne during its short existence. They challenge comparison with those of any discipline whatever. We have lived scarcely a hundred years, we English scholars. In that time we have given our country the greatest dictionary in the world. We have put into print a vast body of mediaeval literature hitherto imprisoned in manuscript. We have established the text of Shakespeare. We have interpreted that of Chaucer. We have transmitted to our most recent poets the influence of our most ancient. We can claim as our own the rich humanity of Raleigh, the more astringent genius of W. P. Ker, the patient wisdom of R. W. Chambers, and (further back) such tough old giants as Skeat, Furnivall, York Powell, Joseph Wright. More recently at Cambridge we have begun an enquiry into the nature of literary experience which has no real precedent later than Aristotle. Most recently of all, at Oxford, we have (first of all Faculties in all

---

[1] Sir Launcelot of the Arthurian Romances; Baron Bradwardine in Sir Walter Scott's *Waverley* (1814); Terence Mulvaney is one of the three privates in Rudyard Kipling's *Soldiers Three* (1888).

[2] Sir Philip Sidney, *The Arcadia* (1590), Book V.

Universities) conducted an Examination for Englishmen now behind barbed wire in Germany. We felt, as we read and re-read the answers, which told of so many hours usefully and delightedly passed in prison, that the labour had been immensely worth while. Here, we thought, was an incontestable witness to the value, not simply of 'appreciation', but of a steady march down centuries of changing sentiment, thought, and manners. Here, we thought, was a good augury for the future. We did not yet know that our prize, like Launcelot's, was death.

The Board of Education carries heavier metal than those who are merely scholars and Englishmen. If it resolves to sink us, it can. But it is desirable that a rather larger public should know what exactly it is that is going down.

10 Meditation in a Toolshed (1945)

I was standing today in the dark toolshed. The sun was shining outside and through the crack at the top of the door there came a sunbeam. From where I stood that beam of light, with the specks of dust floating in it, was the most striking thing in the place. Everything else was almost pitch-black. I was seeing the beam, not seeing things by it.

Then I moved, so that the beam fell on my eyes. Instantly the whole previous picture vanished. I saw no toolshed, and (above all) no beam. Instead I saw, framed in the irregular cranny at the top of the door, green leaves moving on the branches of a tree outside and beyond that, ninety-odd million miles away, the sun. Looking along the beam, and looking at the beam are very different experiences.

But this is only a very simple example of the difference between looking at and looking along. A young man meets a girl. The whole world looks different when he sees her. Her voice reminds him of something he has been trying to remember all his life, and ten minutes' casual chat with her is more precious than all the favours that all other women in the world could grant. He is, as they say, 'in love'. Now comes a scientist and describes this young man's experience from the outside. For him it is all an affair of the young man's genes and a recognized biological stimulus. That is the difference between looking *along* the sexual impulse and looking *at* it.

When you have got into the habit of making this distinction you will find examples of it all day long. The mathematician sits

53

thinking, and to him it seems that he is contemplating timeless and spaceless truths about quantity. But the cerebral physiologist, if he could look inside the mathematician's head, would find nothing timeless and spaceless there – only tiny movements in the grey matter. The savage dances in ecstasy at midnight before Nyonga and feels with every muscle that his dance is helping to bring the new green crops and the spring rain and the babies. The anthropologist, observing that savage, records that he is performing a fertility ritual of the type so-and-so. The girl cries over her broken doll and feels that she has lost a real friend; the psychologist says that her nascent maternal instinct has been temporarily lavished on a bit of shaped and coloured wax.

As soon as you have grasped this simple distinction, it raises a question. You get one experience of a thing when you look along it and another when you look at it. Which is the 'true' or 'valid' experience? Which tells you most about the thing? And you can hardly ask that question without noticing that for the last fifty years or so everyone has been taking the answer for granted. It has been assumed without discussion that if you want the true account of religion you must go, not to religious people, but to anthropologists; that if you want the true account of sexual love you must go, not to lovers, but to psychologists; that if you want to understand some 'ideology' (such as medieval chivalry or the nineteenth-century idea of a 'gentleman'), you must listen not to those who lived inside it, but to sociologists.

The people who look *at* things have had it all their own way; the people who look *along* things have simply been brow-beaten. It has even come to be taken for granted that the external account of a thing somehow refutes or 'debunks' the account given from inside. 'All these moral ideas which look so transcendental and beautiful from inside', says the wiseacre, 'are really only a mass of biological instincts and inherited taboos.' And no one plays the game the other way round by replying, 'If you will only step inside, the things that look to you like instincts and taboos will suddenly reveal their real and transcendental nature.'

That, in fact, is the whole basis of the specifically 'modern' type of thought. And is it not, you will ask, a very sensible basis? For, after all, we are often deceived by things from the inside. For example, the girl who looks so wonderful while we're in love, may really be a very plain, stupid and disagreeable person. The savage's dance to Nyonga does not really cause the crops to grow. Having been so often deceived by looking along, are we not well advised to trust only to looking at? – in fact, to discount all these inside experiences?

Well, no. There are two fatal objections to discounting them *all*. And the first is this. You discount them in order to think more accurately. But you can't think at all – and therefore, of course, can't think accurately – if you have nothing to think *about*. A physiologist, for example, can study pain and find out that it 'is' (whatever *is* means) such and such neural events. But the word *pain* would have no meaning for him unless he had 'been inside' by actually suffering. If he had never looked *along* pain he simply wouldn't know what he was looking *at*. The very subject for his inquiries from outside exists for him only because he has, at least once, been inside.

This case is not likely to occur, because every man has felt pain. But it is perfectly easy to go on all your life giving explanations of religion, love, morality, honour and the like, without having been inside any of them. And if you do that, you are simply playing with counters. You go on explaining a thing without knowing what it is. That is why a great deal of contemporary thought is, strictly speaking, thought about nothing – all the apparatus of thought busily working in a vacuum.

The other objection is this: let us go back to the toolshed. I might have discounted what I saw when looking along the beam (i.e., the leaves moving and the sun) on the ground that it was 'really only a strip of dusty light in a dark shed'. That is, I might have set up as 'true' my 'side vision' of the beam. But then that side vision is itself an instance of the activity we call seeing. And this new instance could also be looked at from outside. I could allow a scientist to tell me that what seemed to be a beam of light in a shed was 'really only an agitation of my own optic nerves'. And that would be just as good (or as bad) a bit of debunking as the previous one. The picture of the beam in the toolshed would now have to be discounted just as the previous picture of the trees and the sun had been discounted. And then, where are you?

In other words, you can step outside one experience only by stepping inside another. Therefore, if all inside experiences are misleading, we are always misled. The cerebral physiologist may say, if he chooses, that the mathematician's thought is 'only' tiny physical movements of the grey matter. But then what about the cerebral physiologist's own thought at that very moment? A second physiologist, looking at it, could pronounce it also to be only tiny physical movements in the first physiologist's skull. Where is the rot to end?

The answer is that we must never allow the rot to begin. We must, on pain of idiocy, deny from the very outset the idea that looking *at* is, by its own nature, intrinsically truer or better than looking *along*. One must look both *along* and *at* everything. In particular cases we shall find reason for regarding the one or the other vision as inferior. Thus the inside vision of rational thinking must be truer than the outside vision which sees only movements of the grey matter; for if the outside vision were the correct one all thought (including this thought itself) would be valueless, and this is self-contradictory. You cannot have a proof that no proofs matter. On the other hand, the inside vision of the savage's dance to Nyonga may be found deceptive because we find reason to believe that crops and babies are not really affected by it. In fact, we must take each case on its merits. But we must start with no prejudice for or against either kind of looking. We do not know in advance whether the lover or the psychologist is giving the more correct account of love, or whether both accounts are equally correct in different ways, or whether both are equally wrong. We just have to find out. But the period of brow-beating has got to end.

11 Hedonics (1945)

There are some pleasures which are almost impossible to account for and very difficult to describe. I have just experienced one of them while travelling by tube from Paddington to Harrow. Whether I can succeed in making it imaginable to you is doubtful; but certainly my only chance of success depends on impressing you, from the outset, with the fact that I am what used to be called a country cousin. Except for a short spell in a London hospital during the last war I have never lived in London. As a result I not only know it badly but also I have never learned to regard it as a quite ordinary place. When, on the return from one of my visits, I plunge underground to reach Paddington, I never know whether I shall strike daylight again at the staircase which comes up under the hotel or at a quite different place out near the end of the departure platforms. 'All is fortune' so far as I am concerned; I have to be prepared for either event as I have to be prepared for fog, rain, or sunshine.

But of all London the most complete *terra incognita* is the suburbs. Swiss Cottage or Maida Vale are to me, if not exactly names like Samarkand or Orgunjé, at any rate names like Winnipeg or Tobolsk. That was the first element in my pleasure. Setting out for Harrow, I was at last going to burrow into that mysterious region which is London and yet wholly unlike the London that country cousins know. I was going to the places from which all the Londoners whom one met in streets and buses really came, and to which they all returned. For central London is, in one deep sense of the word, hardly *inhabited*. People stay there (there are, I gather, hotels) but few live there. It is the stage; the dressing-rooms, the green room, all the 'behind the scenes' world is elsewhere – and that was where I was going.

Perhaps I must labour here to convince you that I am not being ironical. I beg you to believe that all these 'vales' and 'woods' and 'parks' which are so ordinary to Londoners are, to my ear, a kind of incantation. I have never been able to understand why the fact of living in the suburbs should be funny or contemptible. Indeed I have been trying on and off for years to complete a poem which (like so many of my poems) has never got beyond the first two lines –

Who damned suburbia?
'I', said Superbia.

There is, indeed, only one way in which a Londoner can come to understand my feeling. If it gives him pleasure to see for a moment how London looks to me, then this pleasure – the pleasure of seeing a thing the wrong way round, which makes the magic of all mirrors – is the very same which I get from the mere idea of the suburbs. For to think of them is to think that something to me so unhomely as London is to other people simply home. The whole pattern turns inside out and upside down.

It was early evening when my journey began. The train was full, but not yet uncomfortably full, of people going home. It is important to insist – you will see why in a moment – that I was under no illusion about them. If any one had asked me whether I supposed them to be specially good people or specially happy or specially clever, I should have replied with a perfectly truthful No. I knew quite well that perhaps not ten per cent of the homes they were returning to would be free, even for that one night, from ill temper, jealousy, weariness, sorrow or anxiety, and yet – I could not help it – the clicking of all those garden gates, the opening of all those front doors, the unanalysable home smell in all those little halls, the hanging up of all those hats, came over my imagination with all the caress of a half-remembered bit of music. There is an extraordinary charm in other people's domesticities. Every lighted house, seen from the road, is magical: every pram or lawn-mower in someone else's garden: all smells or stirs of cookery from the windows of alien kitchens. I intend no cheap sneer at one's own domesticities. The pleasure is, once more, the mirror pleasure – the pleasure of seeing as an outside what is to others an inside, and realizing that you are doing so. Sometimes one plays the game the other way round.

Then other things come in. There was the charm, as we went on, of running out into evening sunlight, but still in a deep gulley – as if the train were swimming in earth instead of either sailing on it like a real train or worming beneath it like a real tube. There was the charm of sudden silence at stations I had never heard of, and where we seemed to stop for a long time. There was the novelty of being in that kind of carriage without a crowd and without artificial light. But I need not try to enumerate all the ingredients. The point is that all these things between them built up for me a degree of happiness which I must not try to assess because, if I did, you would think I was exaggerating.

But wait. 'Built up' is the wrong expression. They did not actually impose this happiness; they offered it. I was free to take it or not as I chose – like distant music which you need not listen to unless you wish, like a delicious faint wind on your face which you can easily ignore. One was invited to surrender to it. And the odd thing is that something inside me suggested that it would be 'sensible' to refuse the invitation; almost that I would be better employed in remembering that I was going to do a job I do not greatly enjoy and that I should have a very tiresome journey back to Oxford. Then I silenced this inward wiseacre. I accepted the invitation – threw myself open to this feathery, impalpable, tingling invitation. The rest of the journey I passed in a state which can be described only as joy.

I record all this not because I suppose that my adventure, simply as mine, is of any general interest, but because I fancy that something of the same sort will have happened to most people. Is it not the fact that the actual quality of life as we live it – the *weather* of the consciousness from moment to moment – is either much more loosely or else very much more subtly connected than we commonly suppose with what is often called our 'real' life? There are, in fact, two lives? In the one come all the things which (if we were eminent people) our biographers would write about, all that we commonly call good and bad fortune and on which we receive congratulations or condolences. But side by side with this, accompanying it all the way like that ghost compartment which we see through the windows of a train at night, there runs something else. We can ignore it if we choose; but it constantly offers to come in. Huge pleasures, never quite expressible in words, sometimes (if we are careless) not even acknowledged or remembered, invade us from that quarter.

Hence the unreasonable happiness which sometimes surprises a man at those very hours which ought, according to all objective rules, to have been most miserable. You will ask me whether it does not cut both ways. Are there not also grim and hideous visitors from that secondary life – inexplicable cloudings when all is going what we call 'well'? I think there are; but, to be frank, I have found them far less numerous. One is more often happy than wretched without apparent cause.

If I am right in thinking that others besides myself experience this occasional and unpredicted offer, this invitation into Eden, I expect to be right also in believing that others know the inner wiseacre, the *Jailer*, who forbids acceptance. This Jailer has all sorts of tricks. When he finds you not worrying in a situation where worry was possible, he tries to convince you that by beginning to worry you can 'do something' to avert the danger. Nine times out of ten this turns out on inspection to be bosh. On other days he becomes very moral: he says it is 'selfish' or 'complacent' of you to be feeling like that – although, at the very moment of his accusation, you may be setting out to render the only service in your power. If he has discovered a certain weak point in you, he will say you are being 'adolescent'; to which I always reply that he's getting terribly middle-aged.

But his favourite line, in these days, is to confuse the issue. He will pretend, if you let him, that the pleasure, say, in other people's domesticities is based on illusion. He will point out to you at great length (evidence never bothers him) that if you went into any one of those houses you would find every sort of skeleton in every cupboard. But he is only trying to muddle you. The pleasure involves, or need involve, no illusion at all. Distant hills look blue. They still look blue even after you have discovered that this particular beauty disappears when you approach them. The fact that they look blue fifteen miles away is just as much a fact as anything else. If we are to be realists, let us have realism all round. It is a mere brute fact that patches of that boyhood, remembered in one's forties at the bidding of some sudden smell or sound, give one (in the forties) an almost unbearable pleasure. The one is as good a fact as the other. Nothing would induce me to return to the age of fourteen: but neither would anything induce me to forgo the exquisite Proustian or Wordsworthian moments in which that part of the past sometimes returns to me.

We have had enough, once and for all, of Hedonism – the gloomy philosophy which says that Pleasure is the only good. But we have hardly yet begun what may be called *Hedonics*, the science or philosophy of Pleasure. And I submit that the first step in Hedonics is to knock the Jailer down and keep the keys henceforward in our own possession. He has dominated our minds for thirty years or so, and specially in the field of literature and literary criticism. He is a sham realist. He accuses all myth and fantasy and romance of wishful thinking: the way to silence him is to be more realist than he – to lay our ears closer to the murmur of life as it actually flows through us at every moment and to discover there all that quivering and wonder and (in a sense) infinity which the literature that he calls realistic omits. For the story which gives us the experience most like the experiences of living is not necessarily the story whose events are most like those in a biography or a newspaper.

12 Christian Apologetics (1945)

Some of you are priests and some are leaders of youth organiza-
tions.[1] I have little right to address either. It is for priests to teach
me, not for me to teach them. I have never helped to organize
youth, and while I was young myself I successfully avoided being
organized. If I address you it is in response to a request so urged
that I came to regard compliance as a matter of Obedience.

I am to talk about Apologetics. Apologetics means of course
Defence. The first question is – what do you propose to defend?
Christianity, of course: and Christianity as understood by the
Church in Wales. And here at the outset I must deal with an
unpleasant business. It seems to the layman that in the Church of
England we often hear from our priests doctrine which is not
Anglican Christianity. It may depart from Anglican Christianity
in either of two ways: (1) It may be so 'broad' or 'liberal' or
'modern' that it in fact excludes any real Supernaturalism and
thus ceases to be Christian at all. (2) It may, on the other hand, be
Roman. It is not, of course, for me to define to you what Anglican Christianity is – I am your pupil, not your teacher. But I
insist that wherever you draw the lines, bounding lines must
exist, beyond which your doctrine will cease either to be Anglican or to be Christian: and I suggest also that the lines come a
great deal sooner than many modern priests think. I think it is

---

[1] This paper was read to an assembly of Anglican priests and youth leaders of
the Church in Wales at Carmarthen during Easter 1945.

your duty to fix the lines clearly in your own minds: and if you wish to go beyond them you must change your profession.

This is your duty not specially as Christians or as priests but as honest men. There is a danger here of the clergy developing a special professional conscience which obscures the very plain moral issue. Men who have passed beyond these boundary lines in either direction are apt to protest that they have come by their unorthodox opinions honestly. In defence of these opinions they are prepared to suffer obloquy and to forfeit professional advancement. They thus come to feel like martyrs. But this simply misses the point which so gravely scandalizes the layman. We never doubted that the unorthodox opinions were honestly held: what we complain of is your continuing your ministry after you have come to hold them. We always knew that a man who makes his living as a paid agent of the Conservative Party may honestly change his views and honestly become a Communist. What we deny is that he can honestly continue to be a Conservative agent and to receive money from one party while he supports the policy of another.

Even when we have thus ruled out teaching which is in direct contradiction to our profession, we must define our task still further. We are to defend Christianity itself – the faith preached by the Apostles, attested by the Martyrs, embodied in the Creeds, expounded by the Fathers. This must be clearly distinguished from the whole of what any one of us may think about God and Man. Each of us has his individual emphasis: each holds, in addition to the Faith, many opinions which seem to him to be consistent with it and true and important. And so perhaps they are. But as apologists it is not our business to defend *them*. We are defending Christianity; not 'my religion'. When we mention our personal opinions we must always make quite clear the difference between them and the Faith itself. St Paul has given us the model in 1 Corinthians 7:25: on a certain point he has 'no commandment of the Lord' but gives 'his judgement'. No one is left in doubt as to the difference in *status* implied.

This distinction, which is demanded by honesty, also gives the apologist a great tactical advantage. The great difficulty is to get modern audiences to realize that you are preaching Christianity solely and simply because you happen to think it *true*; they always suppose you are preaching it because you like it or think it good for society or something of that sort. Now a clearly maintained distinction between what the Faith actually says and what you would like it to have said, or what you understand or what you personally find helpful or think probable, forces your audience to realize that you are tied to your data just as the scientist is tied by the results of the experiments; that you are not just saying what you like. This immediately helps them to realize that what is being discussed is a question about objective fact – not gas about ideals and points of view.

Secondly, this scrupulous care to preserve the Christian message as something distinct from one's own ideas, has one very good effect upon the apologist himself. It forces him, again and again, to face up to those elements in original Christianity which he personally finds obscure or repulsive. He is saved from the temptation to skip or slur or ignore what he finds disagreeable. And the man who yields to that temptation will, of course, never progress in Christian knowledge. For obviously the doctrines which one finds easy are the doctrines which give Christian sanction to truths you already knew. The new truth which you do not know and which you need, must, in the very nature of things, be hidden precisely in the doctrines you least like and least understand. It is just the same here as in science. The phenomenon which is troublesome, which doesn't fit in with the current scientific theories, is the phenomenon which compels reconsideration and thus leads to new knowledge. Science progresses because scientists, instead of running away from such troublesome phenomena or hushing them up, are constantly seeking them out. In the same way, there will be progress in Christian knowledge only as long as we accept the challenge of the difficult or repellent doctrines. A 'liberal' Christianity which considers itself free to alter the Faith whenever the Faith looks perplexing or repellent *must* be completely stagnant. Progress is made only into a *resisting* material.

From this there follows a corollary about the Apologist's private reading. There are two questions he will naturally ask himself. (1) Have I been 'keeping up', keeping abreast of recent movements in theology? (2) Have I *stood firm (super monstratas vias)*[1] amidst all these 'winds of doctrine'?[2] I want to say emphatically that the second question is far the more important of the two. Our upbringing and the whole atmosphere of the world we live in make it certain that our main temptation will be that of yielding to winds of doctrine, not that of ignoring them. We are not at all likely to be hidebound: we are very likely indeed to be the slaves of fashion. If one has to choose between reading the new books and reading the old, one must choose the old: not because they are necessarily better but because they contain precisely those truths of which our own age is neglectful. The standard of permanent Christianity must be kept clear in our minds and it is against that standard that we must test all contemporary thought. In fact, we must at all costs *not* move with the times. We serve One who said, 'Heaven and Earth shall move with the times, but my words shall not move with the times.'[3]

I am speaking, so far, of theological reading. Scientific reading is a different matter. If you know any science it is very desirable

---

[1] The source of this is, I believe, Jeremiah 6:16, '*State super vias et videte, et interrogate de semitis antiquis quae sit via bona, et ambulate in ea*' which is translated 'Stand ye in the ways, and see, and ask for the old paths, where is the good way, and walk therein'.

[2] Ephesians 4:14.

[3] Matthew 24:35; Mark 13:31; Luke 21:33.

that you should keep it up. We have to answer the current scientific attitude towards Christianity, not the attitude which scientists adopted one hundred years ago. Science is in continual change and we must try to keep abreast of *it*. For the same reason, we must be very cautious of snatching at any scientific theory which, for the moment, seems to be in our favour. We may *mention* such things; but we must mention them lightly and without claiming that they are more than 'interesting'. Sentences beginning 'Science has now proved' should be avoided. If we try to base our apologetic on some recent development in science, we shall usually find that just as we have put the finishing touches to our argument science has changed its mind and quietly withdrawn the theory we have been using as our foundation stone. *Timeo Danaos et dona ferentes*[1] is a sound principle.

While we are on the subject of science, let me digress for a moment. I believe that any Christian who is qualified to write a good popular book on any science may do much more good by that than by any directly apologetic work. The difficulty we are up against is this. We can make people (often) attend to the Christian point of view for half an hour or so; but the moment they have gone away from our lecture or laid down our article, they are plunged back into a world where the opposite position is taken for granted. Every newspaper, film, novel and text book undermines our work. As long as that situation exists, widespread success is simply impossible. We must attack the enemy's line of communication. What we want is not more little books about Christianity, but more little books by Christians on other subjects - with their Christianity *latent*. You can see this most easily if you look at it the other way round. Our Faith is not very likely to be shaken by any book on Hinduism. But if whenever we read an elementary book on Geology, Botany, Politics or

---

[1] I fear the Greeks even when they bear gifts. Virgil, *Aeneid*, Bk. II, line 49.

Astronomy, we found that its implications were Hindu, that would shake us. It is not the books written in direct defence of Materialism that make the modern man a materialist; it is the materialistic assumptions in all the other books. In the same way, it is not books on Christianity that will really trouble him. But he would be troubled if, whenever he wanted a cheap popular introduction to some science, the best work on the market was always by a Christian. The first step to the reconversion of this country is a series, produced by Christians, which can beat the *Penguins* and the *Thinkers' Library* on their own ground. Its Christianity would have to be latent, not explicit: and *of course* its science perfectly honest. Science *twisted* in the interests of apologetics would be sin and folly. But I must return to my immediate subject.

Our business is to present that which is timeless (the same yesterday, today and tomorrow)[1] in the particular language of our own age. The bad preacher does exactly the opposite: he takes the ideas of our own age and tricks them out in the traditional language of Christianity. Thus, for example, he may think about the Beveridge Report[2] and *talk* about the coming of the Kingdom. The core of his thought is merely contemporary; only the superficies is traditional. But your teaching must be timeless at its heart and wear a modern dress.

This raises the question of Theology and Politics. The nearest I can get to a settlement of the frontier problem between them is this: that Theology teaches us what ends are desirable and what means are lawful, while Politics teaches what means are effective. Thus Theology tells us that every man ought to have a decent wage. Politics tells by what means this is likely to be attained.

---

[1] Hebrews 8:8.
[2] Sir William H. Beveridge, *Social Insurance and Allied Services*, Command Paper 6404, Parliamentary Session 1942–43 (London: H.M. Stationery Office, 1942). The 'Beveridge Report' is a plan for the present Social Security system in Britain.

Theology tells us which of these means are consistent with justice and charity. On the political question guidance comes not from Revelation but from natural prudence, knowledge of complicated facts and ripe experience. If we have these qualifications we may, of course, state our political opinions: but then we must make it quite clear that we are giving our personal judgement and have no command from the Lord. Not many priests have these qualifications. Most political sermons teach the congregation nothing except what newspapers are taken at the Rectory.

Our great danger at present is lest the Church should continue to practise a merely missionary technique in what has become a missionary situation. A century ago our task was to edify those who had been brought up in the Faith: our present task is chiefly to convert and instruct infidels. Great Britain is as much part of the mission field as China. Now if you were sent to the Bantus you would be taught their language and traditions. You need similar teaching about the language and mental habits of your own uneducated and unbelieving fellow countrymen. Many priests are quite ignorant on this subject. What I know about it I have learned from talking in RAF camps. They were mostly inhabited by Englishmen and, therefore, some of what I shall say may be irrelevant to the situation in Wales. You will sift out what does not apply.

(1) I find that the uneducated Englishman is an almost total sceptic about History. I had expected he would disbelieve the gospels because they contain miracles: but he really disbelieves them because they deal with things that happened 2,000 years ago. He would disbelieve equally in the battle of Actium if he heard of it. To those who have had our kind of education, his state of mind is very difficult to realize. To us the Present has always appeared as one section in a huge continuous process. In his mind the Present occupies almost the whole field of vision. Beyond it, isolated from it, and quite unimportant, is something called 'The Old Days' – a small, comic jungle in which highway

men, Queen Elizabeth, knights-in-armour, etc., wander about. Then (strangest of all) beyond The Old Days comes a picture of 'Primitive Man'. He is 'science', not 'history', and is therefore felt to be much more real than The Old Days. In other words, the Pre-historic is much more believed in than the Historic.

(2) He has a distrust (very rational in the state of his knowledge) of ancient texts. Thus a man has sometimes said to me, 'These records were written in the days before printing, weren't they? and you haven't got the original bit of paper, have you? So what it comes to is that someone wrote something and someone else copied it and someone else copied *that* and so on. Well, by the time it comes to us, it won't be in the least like the original.' This is a difficult objection to deal with because one cannot, there and then, start teaching the whole science of textual criticism. But at this point their real religion (i.e. faith in 'science') has come to my aid. The assurance that there is a 'science' called 'Textual Criticism' and that its results (not only as regards the New Testament, but as regards ancient texts in general) are generally accepted, will usually be received without objection. (I need hardly point out that the word 'text' must not be used, since to your audience it means only 'a scriptural quotation'.)

(3) A sense of sin is almost totally lacking. Our situation is thus very different from that of the Apostles. The Pagans (and still more the *metuentes*[1]) to whom they preached were haunted by a sense of guilt and to them the Gospel was, therefore, 'good news'. We address people who have been trained to believe that whatever goes wrong in the world is someone else's fault – the Capitalists', the Government's, the Nazis', the Generals', etc. They approach God Himself as His *judges*. They want to know,

---

[1] The *metuentes* or 'god-fearers' were a class of Gentiles who worshipped God without submitting to circumcision and the other ceremonial obligations of the Jewish Law. See Psalm 118:4 and Acts 10:2.

not whether they can be acquitted for sin, but whether He can be acquitted for creating such a world.

In attacking this fatal insensibility it is useless to direct attention *(a)* to sins your audience do not commit, or *(b)* to things they do, but do not regard as sins. They are usually not drunkards. They are mostly fornicators, but then they do not feel fornication to be wrong. It is, therefore, useless to dwell on either of these subjects. (Now that contraceptives have removed the obviously *uncharitable* element in fornication I do not myself think we can expect people to recognize it as a sin until they have accepted Christianity as a whole.)

I cannot offer you a water-tight technique for awaking the sense of sin. I can only say that, in my experience, if one begins from the sin that has been one's own chief problem during the last week, one is very often surprised at the way this shaft goes home. But whatever method we use, our continual effort must be to get their mind away from public affairs and 'crime' and bring them down to brass tacks – to the whole network of spite, greed, envy, unfairness and conceit in the lives of 'ordinary decent people' like themselves (and ourselves).

(4) We must learn the language of our audience. And let me say at the outset that it is no use at all laying down *a priori* what the 'plain man' does or does not understand. You have to find out by experience. Thus most of us would have supposed that the change from 'may truly and indifferently minister justice' to 'may truly and impartially'[1] made that place easier to the uneducated; but a priest of my acquaintance discovered that his sexton saw no difficulty in *indifferently* ('It means making no difference between one man and another' he said) but had no idea what *impartially* meant.

---

[1] The first quotation is from prayer for the 'Whole state of Christ's Church' in the service of Holy Communion, Prayer Book (1662). The second is the revised form of that same phrase as found in the 1928 Prayer Book.

On this question of language the best thing I can do is to make a list of words which are used by the people in a sense different from ours.

ATONEMENT. Does not really exist in a spoken modern English, though it would be recognized as 'a religious word'. In so far as it conveys any meaning to the uneducated I think it means *compensation*. No one word will express to them what Christians mean by *Atonement*: you must paraphrase.

BEING (noun). Never means merely 'entity' in popular speech. Often it means what we should call a 'personal being' (e.g. a man said to me 'I believe in the Holy Ghost but I don't think He is a being').

CATHOLIC means Papistical.

CHARITY. Means (*a*) alms, (*b*) a 'charitable organization', (*c*) much more rarely – indulgence (i.e. a 'charitable' attitude towards a man is conceived as one that denies or condones his sins, not as one that loves the sinner in spite of them).

CHRISTIAN. Has come to include almost no idea of *belief*. Usually a vague term of approval. The question 'What do you call a Christian?' has been asked of me again and again. The answer they *wish* to receive is 'A Christian is a decent chap who's unselfish, etc.'.

CHURCH. Means (*a*) sacred building, (*b*) the clergy. Does *not* suggest to them the 'company of all faithful people'.[1] Generally used in a bad sense. Direct defence of the Church is part of our duty: but use of the word *Church* where there is no time to defend it alienates sympathy and should be avoided where possible.

CREATIVE. Now means merely 'talented', 'original'. The idea of creation in the theological sense is absent from their minds.

[1] A phrase which occurs in the prayer of 'Thanksgiving' at the end of the service of Holy Communion in the Book of Common Prayer (1662).

CREATURE means 'beast', 'irrational animal'. Such an expression as 'We are only creatures' would almost certainly be misunderstood.

CRUCIFIXION, CROSS, ETC. Centuries of hymnody and religious cant have so exhausted these words that they now very faintly – if at all – convey the idea of execution by torture. It is better to paraphrase; and, for the same reason, to say *flogged* for New Testament *scourged*.[1]

DOGMA. Used by the people only in a bad sense to mean 'unproved assertion delivered in an arrogant manner'.

IMMACULATE CONCEPTION. In the mouth of an uneducated speaker *always* means *Virgin Birth*.

MORALITY means *chastity*.

PERSONAL. I had argued for at least ten minutes with a man about the existence of a 'personal devil' before I discovered that *personal* meant to him *corporeal*. I suspect this of being widespread. When they say they don't believe in a 'personal' God they may often mean only that they are not anthropomorphists.

POTENTIAL. When used at all is used in an engineering sense: *never* means 'possible'.

PRIMITIVE. Means crude, clumsy, unfinished, inefficient. 'Primitive Christianity' would not mean to them at all what it does to you.

SACRIFICE. Has no associations with temple and altar. They are familiar with this word only in the journalistic sense ('The Nation must be prepared for heavy sacrifices').

SPIRITUAL. Means primarily *immaterial, incorporeal*, but with serious confusions from the Christian uses of πνεῦμα.[2] Hence the idea that whatever is 'spiritual' in the sense of 'non-

---

[1] Matthew 27:26; Mark 15:15; John 19:1.
[2] Which means 'spirit', as in 1 Corinthians 14:12.

sensuous' is somehow *better* than anything sensuous: e.g. they don't really believe that envy could be as bad as drunkenness. VULGARITY. Usually means obscenity or 'smut'. There are bad confusions (and not only in uneducated minds) between:

(*a*) The obscene or lascivious: what is calculated to provoke lust.
(*b*) The indecorous: what offends against good taste or propriety.
(*c*) The vulgar proper: what is socially 'low'.
'Good' people tend to think (*b*) as sinful as (*a*), with the result that others feel (*a*) to be just as innocent as (*b*).

To conclude – you must translate every bit of your Theology into the vernacular. This is very troublesome and it means you can say very little in half an hour, but it is essential. It is also of the greatest service to your own thought. I have come to the conviction that if you cannot translate your thoughts into uneducated language, then your thoughts were confused. Power to translate is the test of having really understood one's own meaning. A passage from some theological work for translation into the vernacular ought to be a compulsory paper in every Ordination examination.

I turn now to the question of the actual attack. This may be either emotional or intellectual. If I speak only of the intellectual kind, that is not because I undervalue the other but because, not having been given the gifts necessary for carrying it out, I cannot give advice about it. But I wish to say most emphatically that where a speaker has that gift, the direct evangelical appeal of the 'Come to Jesus' type can be as overwhelming today as it was a hundred years ago. I have seen it done, preluded by a religious film and accompanied by hymn singing, and with very remarkable effect. I cannot do it: but those who can ought to do it with all their might. I am not sure that the ideal missionary team ought not to consist of one who argues and one who (in the fullest sense of the word) preaches. Put up your arguer first to undermine their intellectual prejudices; then let the evangelist proper launch his appeal. I have seen this done with great success. But here I must concern myself only with the intellectual attack. *Non omnia possumus omnes.*[1]

And first, a word of encouragement. Uneducated people are not irrational people. I have found that they will endure, and can follow, quite a lot of sustained argument if you go slowly. Often, indeed, the novelty of it (for they have seldom met it before) delights them.

Do not attempt to water Christianity down. There must be no pretence that you can have it with the Supernatural left out. So far as I can see Christianity is precisely the one religion from which the miraculous cannot be separated. You must frankly argue for supernaturalism from the very outset.

The two popular 'difficulties' you will probably have to deal with are these.

(1) 'Now that we know how huge the universe is and how insignificant the Earth, it is ridiculous to believe that the universal God should be specially interested in our concerns.' In answer to this you must first correct their error about *fact*. The insignificance of Earth in relation to the universe is not a modern discovery: nearly 2,000 years ago Ptolemy *(Almagest,* Bk. 1, ch. v) said that in relation to the distance of the fixed stars Earth must be treated as a mathematical point without magnitude. Secondly, you should point out that Christianity says what God has done for Man; it doesn't say (because it doesn't know) what He has or has not done in other parts of the universe. Thirdly, you might recall the parable of the one lost sheep.[2] If Earth has been specially sought by God (which we don't know) that may not

---

[1] Not all things can we all do. Virgil, *Eclogues,* Bk. VIII, line 63.
[2] Matthew 18:11–14; Luke 15:4–7.

imply that it is the most important thing in the universe, but only that it has *strayed*. Finally, challenge the whole tendency to identify size and importance. Is an elephant more important than a man, or a man's leg than his brain?

(2) 'People believed in miracles in the Old Days because they didn't then know that they were contrary to the Laws of Nature.' But they did. If St Joseph didn't know that a virgin birth was contrary to Nature (i.e. if he didn't yet know the normal origin of babies) why, on discovering his wife's pregnancy, was he 'minded to put her away'?[1] Obviously, no event would be recorded as a wonder *unless* the recorders knew the natural order and saw that this was an exception. If people didn't know that the Sun rose in the East they wouldn't be even interested in its once rising in the West. They would not record it as a *miraculum* – nor indeed record it at all. The very idea of 'miracle' presupposes knowledge of the Laws of Nature; you can't have the idea of an exception until you have the idea of a rule.

It is very difficult to produce arguments on the popular level for the existence of God. And many of the most popular arguments seem to me invalid. Some of these may be produced in discussion by friendly members of the audience. This raises the whole problem of the 'embarrassing supporter'. It is brutal (and dangerous) to repel him; it is often dishonest to agree with what he says. I usually try to avoid saying anything about the validity of his argument in *itself* and reply, 'Yes. That may do for you and me. But I'm afraid if we take that line our friend here on my left might say, etc., etc.'

Fortunately, though very oddly, I have found that people are usually disposed to hear the divinity of Our Lord discussed *before* going into the existence of God. When I began I used, if I were giving two lectures, to devote the first to mere Theism; but

[1] Matthew 1:19.

I soon gave up this method because it seemed to arouse little interest. The number of clear and determined Atheists is apparently not very large.

When we come to the Incarnation itself, I usually find that some form of the *aut Deus aut malus homo*[1] can be used. The majority of them started with the idea of the 'great human teacher' who was deified by His superstitious followers. It must be pointed out how very improbable this is among Jews and how different to anything that happened with Plato, Confucius, Buddha, Muhammad. The Lord's own words and claims (of which many are quite ignorant) must be forced home. (The whole case, on a popular level, is very well put indeed in Chesterton's *The Everlasting Man.*)

Something will usually have to be said about the historicity of the gospels. You who are trained theologians will be able to do this in ways which I could not. My own line was to say that I was a professional literary critic and I thought I did know the difference between legend and historical writing: that the gospels were certainly not legends (in one sense they're not *good* enough): and that if they are not history then they are realistic prose fiction of a kind which actually never existed before the eighteenth century. Little episodes such as Jesus writing in the dust when they brought Him the woman taken in adultery[2] (which have no *doctrinal* significance at all) are the mark.

One of the great difficulties is to keep before the audience's mind the question of Truth. They always think you are recommending Christianity not because it is *true* but because it is *good*. And in the discussion they will at every moment try to escape from the issue 'True – or False' into stuff about a good society, or morals, or the incomes of Bishops, or the Spanish Inquisition, or

[1] Either God or a bad man.
[2] John 8:3–8.

78

France, or Poland – or anything whatever. You have to keep forc-
ing them back, and again back, to the real point. Only thus will
you be able to undermine (*a*) Their belief that a certain amount
of 'religion' is desirable but one mustn't carry it too far. One
must keep on pointing out that Christianity is a statement which,
if false, is of *no* importance, and, if true, of infinite importance.
The one thing it cannot be is moderately important. (*b*) Their
firm belief of Article XVIII.[1] Of course it should be pointed out
that, though all salvation is through Jesus, we need not conclude
that He cannot save those who have not explicitly accepted Him
in this life. And it should (at least in my judgement) be made
clear that we are not pronouncing all other religions to be totally
false, but rather saying that in Christ whatever is true in all religions is consummated and perfected. But, on the other hand, I
think we must attack wherever we meet it the nonsensical idea
that mutually exclusive propositions about God can both be true.

For my own part, I have sometimes told my audience that the
only two things really worth considering are Christianity and
Hinduism. (Islam is only the greatest of the Christian heresies,
Buddhism only the greatest of the Hindu heresies. Real Paganism is dead. All that was best in Judaism and Platonism survives
in Christianity.) There isn't really, for an adult mind, this infinite
variety of religions to consider. We may *salva reverentia*[2] divide
religions, as we do soups, into 'thick' and 'clear'. By Thick I
mean those which have orgies and ecstasies and mysteries and
local attachments: Africa is full of Thick religions. By Clear I
mean those which are philosophical, ethical and universalizing:

---

[1] Article XVIII in the Prayer Book: Of *obtaining eternal Salvation only by the
Name of Christ,* which says 'They also are to be had accursed that presume to
say, That every man shall be saved by the Law or Sect which he professeth,
so that he be diligent to frame his life according to that Law, and the light of
Nature. For holy Scripture doth set out unto us only the Name of Jesus
Christ, whereby men must be saved.'

[2] Without outraging reverence.

Stoicism, Buddhism and the Ethical Church are Clear religions. Now if there is a true religion it must be both Thick and Clear: for the true God must have made both the child and the man, both the savage and the citizen, both the head and the belly. And the only two religions that fulfil this condition are Hinduism and Christianity. But Hinduism fulfils it imperfectly. The Clear religion of the Brahmin hermit in the jungle and the Thick religion of the neighbouring temple go on *side by side*. The Brahmin hermit doesn't bother about the temple prostitution, nor the worshipper in the temple about the hermit's metaphysic. But Christianity really breaks down the middle wall of the partition. It takes a convert from central Africa and tells him to obey an enlightened universalist ethic: it takes a twentieth-century academic prig like me and tells me to go fasting to a Mystery, to drink the blood of the Lord. The savage convert has to be Clear: I have to be Thick. That is how one knows one has come to the real religion.

One last word. I have found that nothing is more dangerous to one's own faith than the work of an apologist. No doctrine of that Faith seems to me so spectral, so unreal as one that I have just successfully defended in a public debate. For a moment, you see, it has seemed to rest on oneself: as a result, when you go away from that debate, it seems no stronger than that weak pillar. That is why we apologists take our lives in our hands and can be saved only by falling back continually from the web of our own arguments, as from our intellectual counters, into the Reality – from Christian apologetics into Christ Himself. That also is why we need one another's continual help – *oremus pro invicem*.[1]

---

[1] Let us pray for each other.

13 The Decline of Religion (1946)

From what I see of junior Oxford at present it would be quite easy to draw opposite conclusions about the religious predicament of what we call 'the rising generation', though in reality the undergraduate body includes men and women almost as much divided from one another in age, outlook and experience as they are divided from the dons. Plenty of evidence can be produced to show that religion is in its last decline among them, or that a revival of interest in religion is one of their most noticeable characteristics. And in fact something that may be called 'a decline' and something that may be called 'a revival' are both going on. It will be perhaps more useful to attempt to understand both than to try our luck at 'spotting the winner'.

The 'decline of religion' so often lamented (or welcomed) is held to be shown by empty chapels. Now it is quite true that chapels which were full in 1900 are empty in 1946. But this change was not gradual. It occurred at the precise moment when chapel ceased to be compulsory. It was not in fact a decline; it was a precipice. The sixty men who had come because chapel was a little later than 'rollers'[1] (its only alternative) came no more; the five Christians remained. The withdrawal of

---

[1] After there came to be a number of non-Anglican students in the Oxford colleges, those students who did not wish to attend the morning chapel service were required to report to the Dean five or ten minutes before the service and have their names put on his roll-call. Thus the 'rollers' who did not go to chapel had to be up before those who did go. Neither chapel service nor the Dean's roll-call is compulsory now.

compulsion did not create a new religious situation, but only revealed the situation which had long existed. And this is typical of the 'decline in religion' all over England.

In every class and every part of the country the visible practice of Christianity has grown very much less in the last fifty years. This is often taken to show that the nation as a whole has passed from a Christian to a secular outlook. But if we judge the nineteenth century from the books it wrote, the outlook of our grandfathers (with a very few exceptions) was quite as secular as our own. The novels of Meredith, Trollope and Thackeray are not written either by or for men who see this world as the vestibule of eternity, who regard pride as the greatest of the sins, who desire to be poor in spirit, and look for a supernatural salvation. Even more significant is the absence from Dickens' *Christmas Carol* of any interest in the Incarnation. Mary, the Magi, and the Angels are replaced by 'spirits' of his own invention, and the animals present are not the ox and ass in the stable but the goose and turkey in the poulterer's shop. Most striking of all is the thirty-third chapter of *The Antiquary*, where Lord Glenallan forgives old Elspeth for her intolerable wrong. Glenallan has been painted by Scott as a life-long penitent and ascetic, a man whose every thought has been for years fixed on the supernatural. But when he has to forgive, no motive of a Christian kind is brought into play: the battle is won by 'the generosity of his nature'. It does not occur to Scott that his fasts, his solitudes, his beads and his confessor, however useful as romantic 'properties', could be effectively connected with a serious action which concerns the plot of the book.

I am anxious here not to be misunderstood. I do not mean that Scott was not a brave, generous, honourable man and a glorious writer. I mean that in his work, as in that of most of his contemporaries, only secular and natural values are taken seriously. Plato and Virgil are, in that sense, nearer to Christianity than they.

Thus the 'decline of religion' becomes a very ambiguous phenomenon. One way of putting the truth would be that the religion which has declined was not Christianity. It was a vague Theism with a strong and virile ethical code, which, far from standing over against the 'World', was absorbed into the whole fabric of English institutions and sentiment and therefore demanded churchgoing as (at best) a part of loyalty and good manners or (at worst) a proof of respectability. Hence a social pressure, like the withdrawal of the compulsion, did not create a new situation. The new freedom first allowed accurate observations to be made. When no man goes to church except because he seeks Christ the number of actual believers can at last be discovered. It should be added that this new freedom was partly caused by the very conditions which it revealed. If the various anti-clerical and anti-theistic forces at work in the nineteenth century had had to attack a solid phalanx of radical Christians the story might have been different. But mere 'religion' – morality tinged with emotion', 'what a man does with his solitude', 'the religion of all good men' – has little power of resistance. It is not good at saying No.

The decline of 'religion', thus understood, seems to me in some ways a blessing. At the very worst it makes the issue clear. To the modern undergraduate Christianity is, at least, one of the intellectual options. It is, so to speak, on the agenda: it can be discussed, and a conversion may follow. I can remember times when this was much more difficult. 'Religion' (as distinct from Christianity) was too vague to be discussed ('too sacred to be lightly mentioned') and so mixed up with sentiment and good form as to be one of the embarrassing subjects. If it had to be spoken of, it was spoken of in a hushed, medical voice. Something of the shame of the Cross is, and ought to be, irremovable. But the merely social and sentimental embarrassment is gone. The fog of 'religion' has lifted; the positions and numbers of both armies can be observed; and real shooting is now possible.

The decline of 'religion' is no doubt a bad thing for the 'World'. By it all the things that made England a fairly happy country are, I suppose, endangered: the comparative purity of her public life, the comparative humanity of her police, and the possibility of some mutual respect and kindness between political opponents. But I am not clear that it makes conversions to Christianity rarer or more difficult: rather the reverse. It makes the choice more unescapable. When the Round Table is broken every man must follow either Galahad or Mordred: middle things are gone.

So much for the Decline of Religion; now for a Christian Revival. Those who claim that there is such a Revival would point to the success (I mean success in the sense that it can be tested by sales) of several explicitly and even violently Christian writers, the apparent popularity of lectures on theological subjects, and the brisk atmosphere of not unfriendly discussion on them in which we live. They point, in fact, to what I have heard described as 'the high-brow Christian racket'. It is difficult to describe the phenomenon in quite neutral terms: but perhaps no one would deny that Christianity is now 'on the map' among the younger *intelligentsia* as it was not, say, in 1920. Only freshmen now talk as if the anti-Christian position were self-evident. The days of 'simple un-faith' are as dead as those of 'simple faith'.

At this those who are on the same side as myself are quite properly pleased. We have cause to give thanks: and the comments which I have to add proceed, I hope, not from a natural middle-aged desire to pour cold water into any soup within reach, but only from a desire to forestall, and therefore to disarm, possible disappointments.

In the first place, it must be admitted by anyone who accepts Christianity, that an increased interest in it, or even a growing measure of intellectual assent to it, is a very different thing from the conversion of England or even of a single soul. Conversion requires an alteration of the will, and an alteration which, in the last resort, does not occur without the intervention of the supernatural. I do not in the least agree with those who therefore conclude that the spread of an intellectual (and imaginative) climate favourable to Christianity is useless. You do not prove munition workers useless by showing that they cannot themselves win battles, however proper this reminder would be if they attempted to claim the honour due to fighting men. If the intellectual climate is such that, when a man comes to the crisis at which he must either accept or reject Christ, his reason and imagination are not on the wrong side, then his conflict will be fought out under favourable conditions. Those who help to produce and spread such a climate are therefore doing useful work: and yet no such great matter after all. Their share is a modest one; and it is always possible that nothing – nothing whatever – may come of it. Far higher than they stands that character whom, to the best of my knowledge, the present Christian movement has not yet produced – the *Preacher* in the full sense, the Evangelist, the man on fire, the man who infects. The propagandist, the apologist, only represents John Baptist: the Preacher represents the Lord Himself. He will be sent – or else he will not. But unless he comes we mere Christian intellectuals will not effect very much. That does not mean we should down tools.

In the second place we must remember that a widespread and lively interest in a subject is precisely what we call a Fashion. And it is the nature of Fashions not to last. The present Christian movement may, or may not, have a long run ahead of it. But sooner or later it must lose the public ear; in a place like Oxford such changes are extraordinarily rapid. Bradley and the other idealists fell in a few terms, the Douglas scheme even more suddenly, the Vorticists overnight.[1] (Who now remembers Pogo?[2] Who now reads *Childermass?*[3]) Whatever in our present success mere fashion has given us, mere fashion will presently withdraw. The real conversions will remain: but nothing else will. In that sense we may be on the brink of a real and permanent Christian revival: but it will work slowly and obscurely and in small groups. The present sunshine (if I may so call it) is certainly temporary. The grain must be got into the barns before the wet weather comes.

This mutability is the fate of all movements, fashions, intellectual climates and the like. But a Christian movement is also up against something sterner than the mere fickleness of taste. We have not yet had (at least in junior Oxford) any really bitter opposition. But if we have many more successes, this will certainly appear. The enemy has not yet thought it worth while to fling his whole weight against us. But he soon will. This happens in the history of every Christian movement, beginning with the Ministry of Christ Himself. At first it is welcome to all who have no special reason for opposing it: at this stage he who is not against it is for it. What men notice is its difference from those aspects of the World which they already dislike. But later on, as the real meaning of the Christian claim becomes apparent, its demand for total surrender, the sheer chasm between Nature and Supernature, men are increasingly 'offended'. Dislike, terror, and finally hatred succeed: none who will not give it what it asks (and

---

[1] F. H. Bradley (1846–1924) was a Fellow of Merton College, Oxford, and the author of *Appearance and Reality* (London, 1893). Major C. H. Douglas, a socio-economist, wrote, among other works, *Social Credit* (London, 1933). The Vorticists were a school of artists of the 1920s.

[2] No one, practically. As far as I can discover, Pogo, or the Pogo-stick, which was invented in 1922, is a stilt with a spring on which the player jumps about.

[3] *Childermass* is by P. Wyndham Lewis (London, 1928).

it asks all) can endure it: all who are not with it are against it. That is why we must cherish no picture of the present intellectual movement simply growing and spreading and finally reclaiming millions by sweet reasonableness. Long before it became as important as that the real opposition would have begun, and to be on the Christian side would be costing a man (at the least) his career. But remember, in England the opposition will quite likely be *called* Christianity (or Christo-democracy, or British Christianity, or something of that kind).

I think – but how should I know? – that all is going reasonably well. But it is early days. Neither our armour nor our enemies' is yet engaged. Combatants always tend to imagine that the war is further on than it really is.

14 Religion Without Dogma?[1] (1946)

In his paper on 'The Grounds of Modern Agnosticism', Professor Price maintains the following positions: (1) That the essence of religion is belief in God and immortality; (2) that in most actual religions the essence is found in connection with 'accretions of dogma and mythology'[2] which have been rendered incredible by the progress of science; (3) that it would be very desirable, if it were possible, to retain the essence purged of the accretions; but (4) that science has rendered the essence almost as hard to believe as the accretions. For the doctrine of immortality involves the dualistic view that man is a composite creature, a soul in a state of symbiosis with a physical organism. But in so far as science can successfully regard man monistically, as a single organism whose psychological properties all arise from his physical, the soul becomes an indefensible hypothesis. In conclusion, Professor Price found our only hope in certain empirical

---

[1] This paper was originally read to the Oxford Socratic Club on 20th May 1946, in answer to a paper of Professor H. H. Price on 'The Grounds of Modern Agnosticism' on 20th October 1944. Both were later published in the *Phoenix Quarterly* (Autumn 1946). Though Lewis's paper was afterwards reprinted in *The Socratic Digest* (1948), it is obvious from the fact that many errors which appear in the *Socratic* version were corrected in the *Quarterly* version, that the *Quarterly* version represents Lewis's final revision. Besides this, I have incorporated in the text given here all the marginal emendations and additions which Lewis made in his own copy of the *Phoenix Quarterly*.

[2] H. H. Price, 'The Grounds of Modern Agnosticism', *Phoenix Quarterly*, Vol. 1, No. 1 (Autumn 1946), p. 25.

evidence for the soul which appears to him satisfactory; in fact, in the findings of Psychical Research.

My disagreement with Professor Price begins, I am afraid, at the threshold. I do not define the essence of religion as belief in God and immortality. Judaism in its earlier stages had no belief in immortality, and for a long time no belief which was religiously relevant. The shadowy existence of the ghost in Sheol was one of which Jehovah took no account and which took no account of Jehovah. In Sheol all things are forgotten. The religion was centred on the ritual and ethical demands of Jehovah in the present life, and also, of course, on benefits expected from Him. These benefits are often merely worldly benefits (grandchildren, and peace upon Israel), but a more specifically religious note is repeatedly struck. The Jew is athirst for the living God,[1] he delights in His Laws as in honey or treasure,[2] he is conscious of himself in Jehovah's presence as unclean of lips and heart.[3] The glory or splendour of the god is worshipped for its own sake. In Buddhism, on the other hand, we find that a doctrine of immortality is central, while there is nothing specifically religious. Salvation from immortality, deliverance from reincarnation, is the very core of its message. The existence of the gods is not necessarily decried, but it is of no religious significance. In Stoicism again both the religious quality and the belief in immortality are variables, but they do not vary in direct ratio. Even within Christianity itself we find a striking expression, not without influence from Stoicism, of the subordinate position of immortality. When Henry More ends a poem on the spiritual life by saying that if, after all, he should turn out to be mortal he would be

[1] Psalm 42:2.
[2] Psalm 19:10.
[3] Isaiah 6:5.

89

. . .Satisfide
A lonesome mortal God t' have dide.[1]

From my own point of view, the examples of Judaism and Buddhism are of immense importance. The system which is meaningless without a doctrine of immortality regards immortality as a nightmare, not as a prize. The religion which, of all ancient religions, is most specifically religious, that is, at once most ethical and most numinous, is hardly interested in the question. Believing as I do, that Jehovah is a real being, indeed the *ens realissimum*, I cannot sufficiently admire the divine tact of thus training the chosen race for centuries in a religion before even hinting the shining secret of eternal life. He behaves like the rich lover in a romance who woos the maiden on his own merits, disguised as a poor man, and only when he has won her reveals that he has a throne and palace to offer. For I cannot help thinking that any religion which begins with a thirst for immortality is damned, as a religion, from the outset. Until a certain spiritual level has been reached, the promise of immortality will always operate as a bribe which vitiates the whole religion and infinitely inflames those very self-regards which religion must cut down and uproot. For the essence of religion, in my view, is the thirst for an end higher than natural ends; the finite self's desire for, and acquiescence in, and self-rejection in favour of, an object wholly good and wholly good for it. That the self-rejection will turn out to be also a self-finding, that bread cast upon the waters will be found after many days, that to die is to live – these are sacred paradoxes of which the human race must not be told too soon.

Differing from Professor Price about the essence of religion, I naturally cannot, in a sense, discuss whether the essence as he

---

[1] 'Resolution', *The Complete Poems of Dr Henry More*, ed. Alexander B. Grosart (Edinburgh, 1878), line 117, p. 176 .

defines it co-exists with accretions of dogma and mythology. But I freely admit that the essence as I define it always co-exists with other things; and that some of these other things even I would call mythology. But my list of things mythological would not coincide with his, and our views of mythology itself probably differ. A great many different views on it have, of course, been held. Myths have been accepted as literally true, then as allegorically true (by the Stoics), as confused history (by Euhemerus),[1] as priestly lies (by the philosophers of the Enlightenment), as imitative agricultural ritual mistaken for propositions (in the days of Frazer).[2] If you start from a naturalistic philosophy, then something like the view of Euhemerus or the view of Frazer is likely to result. But I am not a naturalist. I believe that in the huge mass of mythology which has come down to us a good many different sources are mixed – true history, allegory, ritual, the human delight in story telling, etc. But among these sources I include the supernatural, both diabolical and divine. We need here concern ourselves only with the latter. If my religion is erroneous then occurrences of similar motifs in pagan stories are, of course, instances of the same, or a similar, error. But if my religion is true, then these stories may well be a *preparatio evangelica,* divine hinting in poetic and ritual form at the same central truth which was later focused and (so to speak) historicized in the Incarnation. To me, who first approached Christianity from a delighted interest in, and reverence for, the best pagan imagination, who loved Balder before Christ and Plato before St Augustine, the anthropological argument against Christianity has never been formidable. On the contrary, I could not believe Christianity if I

---

[1] A Sicilian writer (c. 315 B.C.) who developed the theory that the ancient beliefs about the gods originated from the elaboration of traditions of actual historical persons.

[2] James George Frazer, *The Golden Bough* (London, 1922).

were forced to say that there were a thousand religions in the world of which 999 were pure nonsense and the thousandth (fortunately) true. My conversion, very largely, depended on recognizing Christianity as the completion, the actualization, the entelechy, of something that had never been wholly absent from the mind of man. And I still think that the agnostic argument from similarities between Christianity and paganism works only if you know the answer. If you start by knowing on other grounds that Christianity is false, then the pagan stories may be another nail in its coffin: just as if you started by knowing that there were no such things as crocodiles then the various stories about dragons might help to confirm your disbelief. But if the truth or falsehood of Christianity is the very question you are discussing, then the argument from anthropology is surely a *petitio*.

There are, of course, many things in Christianity which I accept as fact and which Professor Price would regard as mythology. In a word, there are miracles. The contention is that science has proved that miracles cannot occur. According to Professor Price 'a Deity who intervened miraculously and suspended natural law could never be accepted by Science';[1] whence he passes on to consider whether we cannot still believe in Theism without miracles. I am afraid I have not understood why the miracles could never be accepted by one who accepted science.

Professor Price bases his view on the nature of scientific method. He says that that method is based on two assumptions. The first is that all events are subject to laws, and he adds: 'It does not matter for our purpose whether the laws are "deterministic" or only "statistical".'[2] But I submit that it matters to the scientist's view of the miraculous. The notion that natural laws may be merely statistical results from the modern belief that the

[1] Price, *op. cit.*, p. 20.
[2] ibid.

individual unit of matter obeys no laws. Statistics were introduced to explain why, despite the lawlessness of the individual unit, the behaviour of gross bodies was regular. The explanation was that, by a principle well known to actuaries, the law of averages levelled out the individual eccentricities of the innumerable units contained in even the smallest gross body. But with this conception of the lawless units the whole impregnability of nineteenth-century Naturalism has, as it seems to me, been abandoned. What is the use of saying that all events are subject to laws if you also say that every event which befalls the individual unit of matter is *not* subject to laws. Indeed, if we define nature as the system of events in space-time governed by interlocking laws, then the new physics has really admitted that something other than nature exists. For if nature means the interlocking system then the behaviour of the individual unit is outside nature. We have admitted what may be called the sub-natural. After that admission what confidence is left us that there may not be a supernatural as well? It may be true that the lawlessness of the little events fed into nature from the sub-natural is always ironed out by the law of averages. It does not follow that great events could not be fed into her by the supernatural: nor that they also would allow themselves to be ironed out.

The second assumption which Professor Price attributes to the scientific method is 'that laws can only be discovered by the study of publicly observable regularities'.[1] Of course they can. This does not seem to me to be an assumption so much as a self-evident proposition. But what is it to the purpose? If a miracle occurs it is by definition an interruption of regularity. To discover a regularity is by definition not to discover its interruptions, even if they occur. You cannot discover a railway accident from studying Bradshaw: only by being there when it happens or

[1] ibid.

hearing about it afterwards from someone who was. You cannot discover extra half-holidays by studying a school timetable: you must wait till they are announced. But surely this does not mean that a student of Bradshaw is logically forced to deny the possibility of railway accidents. This point of scientific method merely shows (what no one to my knowledge ever denied) that if miracles *did* occur, science, as science, would not prove, or disprove, their occurrence. What cannot be trusted to recur is not material for science: that is why history is not one of the sciences. You cannot find out what Napoleon did at the battle of Austerlitz by asking him to come and fight it again in a laboratory with the same combatants, the same terrain, the same weather, and in the same age. You have to go to the records. We have not, in fact, proved that science excludes miracles: we have only proved that the question of miracles, like innumerable other questions, excludes laboratory treatment.

[1][If I thus hand over miracles from science to history (but not, of course, to historians who beg the question by beginning with materialistic assumptions) Professor Price thinks I shall not fare much better. Here I must speak with caution, for I do not profess to be a historian or a textual critic. I would refer you to Sir Arnold Lunn's book *The Third Day*.[2] If Sir Arnold is right, then the biblical criticism which began in the nineteenth century has already shot its bolt, and most of its conclusions have been successfully disputed, though it will, like nineteenth-century materialism, long continue to dominate popular thought. What I can say with more certainty is that that *kind* of criticism – the kind which discovers that every old book was made by six anonymous authors well provided with scissors and paste, and that every

---

[1] In order that nothing should be lost to the reader, I have included between square brackets those portions from the *Socratic* version of this paper which Lewis omitted in revising it for the *Phoenix Quarterly*. See footnote.

[2] (London, 1945).

anecdote of the slightest interest is unhistorical, has already begun to die out in the studies I know best. The period of arbitrary scepticism about the canon and text of Shakespeare is now over: and it is reasonable to expect that this method will soon be used only on Christian documents and survive only in the *Thinkers' Library* and the theological colleges.]

I find myself, therefore, compelled to disagree with Professor Price's second point. I do not think that science has shown, or, by its nature, could ever show that the miraculous element in religion is erroneous. I am not speaking, of course, about the psychological effects of science on those who practise it or read its results. That the continued application of scientific methods breeds a temper of mind unfavourable to the miraculous, may well be the case, but even here there would seem to be some difference among the sciences. Certainly, if we think, not of the miraculous in particular, but of religion in general, there is such a difference. Mathematicians, astronomers and physicists are often religious, even mystical; biologists much less often; economists and psychologists very seldom indeed. It is as their subject matter comes nearer to man himself that their anti-religious bias hardens.

And that brings me to Professor Price's fourth point – for I would rather postpone consideration of his third. His fourth point, it will be remembered, was that science had undermined not only what he regards as the mythological accretions of religion, but also what he regards as its essence. That essence is for him Theism and immortality. In so far as natural science can give a satisfactory account of man as a purely biological entity, it excludes the soul and therefore excludes immortality. That, no doubt, is why the scientists who are most, or most nearly, concerned with man himself are the most anti-religious.

Now most assuredly if naturalism is right then it is at this point, at the study of man himself, that it wins its final victory and overthrows all our hopes: not only our hope of immortality, but our hope of finding significance in our lives here and now. On the other hand, if naturalism is wrong, it will be here that it will reveal its fatal philosophical defect, and that is what I think it does.

On the fully naturalistic view all events are determined by laws. Our logical behaviour, in other words our thoughts, and our ethical behaviour, including our ideals as well as our acts of will, are governed by biochemical laws; these, in turn, by physical laws which are themselves actuarial statements about the lawless movements of matter. These units never intended to produce the regular universe we see: the law of averages (successor to Lucretius's *exiguum clinamen)*[1] has produced it out of the collision of these random variations in movement. The physical universe never intended to produce organisms. The relevant chemicals on earth, and the sun's heat, thus juxtaposed, gave rise to this disquieting disease of matter: organization. Natural selection, operating on the minute differences between one organism and another, blundered into that sort of phosphorescence or mirage which we call consciousness – and that, in some cortexes beneath some skulls, at certain moments, still in obedience to physical laws, but to physical laws now filtered through laws of a more complicated kind, takes the form we call thought. Such, for instance, is the origin of this paper: such was the origin of Professor Price's paper. What we should speak of as his 'thoughts' were merely the last link of a causal chain in which all the previous links were irrational. He spoke as he did because the matter of his brain was behaving in a certain way: and the whole history of the universe up to that moment had forced it to behave in that way. What we called his thought was essentially a phenomenon of the same sort as his other secretions – the form which the vast

[1] small inclination. *De Rerum Natura*, Bk. II, line 292.

irrational process of nature was bound to take at a particular point of space and time.

Of course it did not feel like that to him or to us while it was going on. He appeared to himself to be studying the nature of things, to be in some way aware of the realities, even supersensuous realities, outside his own head. But if strict naturalism is right, he was deluded: he was merely enjoying the conscious reflection of irrationally determined events in his own head. It appeared to him that his thoughts (as he called them) could have to outer realities that wholly immaterial relation which we call truth or falsehood: though, in fact, being but the shadow of cerebral events, it is not easy to see that they could have any relations to the outer world except causal relations. And when Professor Price defended scientists, speaking of their devotion to truth and their constant following of the best light they knew, it seemed to him that he was choosing an attitude in obedience to an ideal. He did not feel that he was merely suffering a reaction determined by ultimately amoral and irrational sources, and no more capable of rightness or wrongness than a hiccup or a sneeze.

It would have been impossible for Professor Price to have written, or us to have read, his paper with the slightest interest if he and we had consciously held the position of strict naturalism throughout. But we can go further. It would be impossible to accept naturalism itself if we really and consistently believed naturalism. For naturalism is a system of thought. But for naturalism all thoughts are mere events with irrational causes. It is, to me at any rate, impossible to regard the thoughts which make up naturalism in that way and, at the same time, to regard them as a real insight into external reality. Bradley distinguished *idea-event* from *idea-making*,[1] but naturalism seems to me committed to

[1] 'Spoken and Written English', *The Collected Papers of Henry Bradley*, ed. Robert Bridges (Oxford, 1928), pp. 168–93.

regarding ideas simply as events. For meaning is a relation of a wholly new kind, as remote, as mysterious, as opaque to empirical study, as soul itself.

Perhaps this may be even more simply put in another way. Every particular thought (whether it is a judgement of fact or a judgement of value) is always and by all men discounted the moment they believe that it can be explained, without remainder, as the result of irrational causes. Whenever you know what the other man is saying is wholly due to his complexes or to a bit of bone pressing on his brain, you cease to attach any importance to it. But if naturalism were true then all thoughts whatever would be wholly the result of irrational causes. Therefore, all thoughts would be equally worthless. Therefore, naturalism is worthless. If it is true, then we can know no truths. It cuts its own throat.

[I remember once being shown a certain kind of knot which was such that if you added one extra complication to make assurance doubly sure you suddenly found that the whole thing had come undone in your hands and you had only a bit of string. It is like that with naturalism. It goes on claiming territory after territory: first the inorganic, then the lower organisms, then man's body, then his emotions. But when it takes the final step and we attempt a naturalistic account of thought itself, suddenly the whole thing unravels. The last fatal step has invalidated all the preceding ones: for they were all reasoning and reason itself has been discredited. We must, therefore, either give up thinking altogether or else begin over again from the ground floor.]

There is no reason, at this point, to bring in either Christianity or spiritualism. We do not need them to refute naturalism. It refutes itself. Whatever else we may come to believe about the universe, at least we cannot believe naturalism. The validity of rational thought, accepted in an utterly non-naturalistic, transcendental (if you will), supernatural sense, is the necessary presupposition of all other theorizing. There is simply no sense in beginning with a view of the universe and trying to fit the claims of thought in at a later stage. By thinking at all we have claimed that our thoughts are more than mere natural events. All other propositions must be fitted in as best they can round that primary claim.

Holding that science has not refuted the miraculous element in religion, much less that naturalism, rigorously taken, can refute anything except itself, I do not, of course, share Professor Price's anxiety to find a religion which can do without what he calls the mythology. What he suggests is simple Theism, rendered credible by a belief in immortality which, in its turn, is guaranteed by Psychical Research. Professor Price is not, of course, arguing that immortality would of itself prove Theism: it would merely remove an obstacle to Theism. The positive source of Theism he finds in religious experience.

At this point it is very important to decide which of two questions we are asking. We may be asking: (1) whether this purged minimal religion suggested by Professor Price is capable, as a historical, social and psychological entity, of giving fresh heart to society, strengthening the moral will, and producing all those other benefits which, it is claimed, the old religions have sometimes produced. On the other hand, we may be asking: (2) whether this minimal religion will be the true one; that is, whether it contains the only true propositions we can make about ultimate questions.

The first question is not a religious question but a sociological one. The religious mind as such, like the older sort of scientific mind as such, does not care a rap about socially useful propositions. Both are athirst for reality, for the utterly objective, for that which is what it is. The 'open mind' of the scientist and the emptied and silenced mind of the mystic are both efforts to eliminate what is our own in order that the Other may speak. And if, turning aside from the religious attitude, we speak for a moment as mere sociologists, we must admit that history does not encourage us to expect much envigorating power in a minimal religion. Attempts at such a minimal religion are not new – from Akhenaton[1] and Julian the Apostate[2] down to Lord Herbert of Cherbury[3] and the late H.G. Wells. But where are the saints, the consolations, the ecstasies? The greatest of such attempts was that simplification of Jewish and Christian traditions which we call Islam. But it retained many elements which Professor Price would regard as mythical and barbaric, and its culture is by no means one of the richest or most progressive.

Nor do I see how such a religion, if it became a vital force, would long be preserved in its freedom from dogma. Is its God to be conceived pantheistically, or after the Jewish, Platonic, Christian fashion? If we are to retain the minimal religion in all its purity, I suppose the right answer would be: 'We don't know, and we must be content not to know.' But that is the end of the minimal religion as a practical affair. For the question is of pressing practical importance. If the God of Professor Price's religion is an impersonal spirituality diffused through the whole universe, equally present, and present in the same mode, at all points of space and time, then He – or It – will certainly be conceived as being beyond good and evil, expressed equally in the

---

[1] Akhenaton (Amenhotep IV), king of Egypt, who came to the throne about 1375 B.C. and introduced a new religion, in which the sun-god Ra (designated as 'Aton') superseded Amon.

[2] Roman emperor A.D. 361–3, who was brought up compulsorily as a Christian, but who on attaining the throne proclaimed himself a pagan. He made a great effort to revive the worship of the old gods.

[3] Edward Herbert (1583–1648). He is known as the 'Father of Deism', for he maintained that among the 'common notions' apprehended by instinct are the existence of God, the duty of worship and repentance, and future rewards and punishment. This 'natural religion', he maintained, had been vitiated by superstition and dogma.

brothel or the torture chamber and in the model factory or the university common room. If, on the other hand, He is a personal Being standing outside His creation, commanding this and prohibiting that, quite different consequences follow. The choice between these two views affects the choice between courses of action at every moment both in private and public life. Nor is this the only such question that arises. Does the minimal religion know whether its god stands in the same relation to all men, or is he related to some as he is not related to others? To be true to its undogmatic character it must again say: 'Don't ask.' But if that is the reply, then the minimal religion cannot exclude the Christian view that He was present in a special way in Jesus, nor the Nazi view that He is present in a special way in the German race, nor the Hindu view that He is specially present in the Brahmin, nor the central African view that He is specially present in the thigh-bone of a dead English Tommy.

All these difficulties are concealed from us as long as the minimal religion exists only on paper. But suppose it were somehow established all over what is left of the British Empire, and let us suppose that Professor Price has (most reluctantly and solely from a sense of duty) become its supreme head on earth. I predict that one of two things must happen: (1) In the first month of his reign he will find himself uttering his first dogmatic definition – he will find himself saying, for example: 'No. God is not an amoral force diffused through the whole universe to whom suttee and temple prostitution are no more and no less acceptable than building hospitals and teaching children; he is a righteous creator, separate from his creation, who demands of you justice and mercy'; or (2) Professor Price will not reply. In the second case is it not clear what will happen? Those who have come to his minimal religion from Christianity will conceive God in the Jewish, Platonic, Christian way; those who have come from Hinduism will conceive Him pantheistically; and the plain men who have come from nowhere will conceive Him as a righteous Creator in their moments of moral indignation, and as a pantheistic God in their moments of self-indulgence. And the ex-Marxist will think He is specially present in the Proletariat, and the ex-Nazi will think he is specially present in the German people. And they will hold world conferences at which they all speak the same language and reach the most edifying agreement: but they will all mean totally different things. The minimal religion in fact cannot, while it remains minimal, be acted on. As soon as you *do* anything you have assumed one of the dogmas. In practice it will not be a religion at all; it will be merely a new colouring given to all the different things people were doing already.

[I submit it to Professor Price, with great respect, that when he spoke of mere Theism, he was all the time unconsciously assuming a particular conception of God: that is, he was assuming a dogma about God. And I do not think he was deducing it solely, or chiefly, from his own religious experience or even from a study of religious experience in general. For religious experience can be made to yield almost any sort of God. I think Professor Price assumed a certain sort of God because he has been brought up in a certain way: because Bishop Butler and Hooker and Thomas Aquinas and Augustine and St Paul and Christ and Aristotle and Plato are, as we say, 'in his blood'. He was not really starting from scratch. Had he done so, had God meant in his mind a being about whom no dogma whatever is held, I doubt whether he would have looked for even social salvation in such an empty concept. All the strength and value of the minimal religion, for him as for all others who accept it, is derived not from it, but from the tradition which he imports into it.]

The minimal religion will, in my opinion, leave us all doing what we were doing before. Now it, in itself, will not be an objection from Professor Price's point of view. He was not working for unity, but for some spiritual dynamism to see us through the black night of civilization. If Psychical Research has the effect of enabling people to continue, or to return to, all the diverse religions which naturalism has threatened, and if they can thus get power and hope and discipline, he will, I believe, leave us – as Western, mechanized, democratic, secularized men – exactly where we were. In what way will a belief in the immortality vouched for by Psychical Research, and in an unknown God, restore to us the virtue and energy of our ancestors? It seems to me that both beliefs, unless reinforced by something else, will be to modern man very shadowy and inoperative. If indeed we knew that God were righteous, that He had purposes for us, that He was the leader in a cosmic battle and that some real issue hung on our conduct in the field, then it would be something to the purpose. Or if, again, the utterances which purport to come from the other world ever had the accent which really *suggests* another world, ever spoke (as even the inferior actual religions do) with that voice before which our mortal nature trembles with awe or joy, then that also would be to the purpose. But the god of minimal Theism remains powerless to excite either fear or love: can be given power to do so only from those traditional resources to which, in Professor Price's conception, science will never permit our return. As for the utterances of the mediums ... I do not wish to be offensive. But will even the most convinced spiritualist claim that one sentence from that source has ever taken its place among the golden sayings of mankind, has ever approached (much less equalled) in power to elevate, strengthen or correct even the second rank of such sayings? Will anyone deny that the vast majority of spirit messages sink pitiably below the best that has been thought and said even in this world? – that in most of them we find a banality and provincialism, a paradoxical union of the prim with the enthusiastic, of flatness and gush, which would suggest that the souls of the moderately respectable are in the keeping of Annie Besant[1] and Martin Tupper?[2]

I am not arguing from the vulgarity of the messages that their claim to come from the dead is false. If I did the spiritualist would reply that this quality is due to imperfections in the medium of communication. Let it be so. We are not here discussing the truth of spiritualism, but its power to become the starting point of a religion. And for that purpose I submit that the poverty of its contents disqualifies it. A minimal religion compounded of spirit messages and bare Theism has no power to touch any of the deepest chords in our nature, or to evoke any response which will raise us even to a higher secular level – let alone to the spiritual life. The god of whom no dogmas are believed is a mere shadow. He will not produce that fear of the Lord in which wisdom begins, and, therefore, will not produce that love in which it is consummated. The immortality which the messages suggest can produce in mediocre spirits only a vague comfort for our unredeemedly personal hankerings, a shadowy sequel to the story of this world in which all comes right (but right in how pitiable a sense!), while the more spiritual will feel that it has added a new horror to death – the horror of mere endless succession, of indefinite imprisonment in that which binds us all, *das Gemeine*.[3] There is in this minimal religion nothing that can convince, convert, or (in the higher sense) console; nothing, therefore, which can restore vitality to our civilization. It is not costly enough. It can never be a controller or even a rival to our natural sloth and greed. A flag, a song, an old school tie, is stronger than

[1] Annie Besant (1847–1933) was an ardent supporter of Liberal causes and became a member of the Theosophical Society in 1889.
[2] Martin Tupper (1810–89) is probably best known for his *Proverbial Philosophy* – commonplace maxims and reflections couched in a rhythmical form.
[3] Johann Wolfgang Goethe, *Epilog zu Schillers Glocke*, 1. 32. '*Das Gemeine*' means something like 'that which dominates us all'.

it; much more, the pagan religions. Rather than pin my hopes on it I would almost listen again to the drum-beat in my blood (for the blood is at least in some sense the life) and join in the song of the Maenads:

> Happy they whom the Daimons
> Have befriended, who have entered
> The divine orgies, making holy
> Their life-days, till the dance throbs
> In their heart-beats, while they romp with
> Dionysus on the mountains ...[1]

Yes, almost; I'd sooner be a pagan suckled in a creed outworn.

Almost, but not, of course, quite. If one is forced to such an alternative, it is perhaps better to starve in a wholly secularized and meaningless universe than to recall the obscenities and cruelties of paganism. They attract because they are a distortion of the truth, and therefore, retain some of its flavour. But with this remark I have passed into our second question. I shall not be expected at the end of this paper to begin an apologetic for the truth of Christianity. I will only say something which in one form or another I have said perhaps too often already. If there is no God then we have no interest in the minimal religion or any other. We will not make a lie even to save civilization. But if there is, then it is so probable as to be almost axiomatic that the initiative lies wholly on His side. If He can be known it will be by self-revelation on His part, not by speculation on ours. We, therefore, look for Him where it is claimed that He has revealed Himself by miracle, by inspired teachers, by enjoined ritual. The traditions conflict, yet the longer and more sympathetically we study them the more we become aware of a common element in many of

---

[1] Euripides, *Bacchae,* line 74.

them: the theme of sacrifice, of mystical communion through the shed blood, of death and rebirth, of redemption, is too clear to escape notice. We are fully entitled to use moral and intellectual criticism. What we are not, in my opinion, entitled to do is simply to abstract the ethical element and set that up as a religion on its own. Rather in that tradition which is at once more completely ethical and most transcends mere ethics – in which the old themes of the sacrifice and re-birth recur in a form which transcends, though there it no longer revolts, our conscience and our reason – we may still most reasonably believe that we have the consummation of all religion, the fullest message from the wholly other, the living creator, who, if He is at all, must be the God not only of the philosophers, but of mystics and savages, not only of the head and heart, but also of the primitive emotions and the spiritual heights beyond all emotion. We may still reasonably attach ourselves to the Church, to the only concrete organization which has preserved down to this present time the core of all the messages, pagan and perhaps pre-pagan, that have ever come from beyond the world, and begin to practise the only religion which rests not upon some selection of certain supposedly 'higher' elements in our nature, but on the shattering and rebuilding, the death and re-birth, of that nature in every part: neither Greek nor Jew nor barbarian, but a new creation.

[Note: *The debate between Lewis and Professor Price did not end here. In* The Socratic Digest, *No. 4 [1948], there follows a 'Reply' to Lewis's 'Religion without Dogma?' by Professor Price (pp. 94–102). Then, at a meeting of the Socratic Club on 2nd February 1948, Miss G. E. M. Anscombe read a paper entitled 'A reply to Mr C. S. Lewis's Argument that "Naturalism is Self-refuting" ', afterwards published in the same issue of the* Digest *(pp. 7–15) as Professor Price's 'Reply'. Miss Anscombe criticized the argument found on pp. 96–9 of the paper printed above as well as Chapter III, 'The*

Self-Contradiction of the Naturalist', of Lewis's book Miracles
*(London, 1947). The two short pieces that follow are (A) the
Socratic minute-book account of Lewis's reply to Miss Anscombe,
and (B) a reply written by Lewis himself – both reprinted from the
same issue of the* Digest *mentioned above (pp. 15–16). Aware that
the third chapter of his* Miracles *was ambiguous, Lewis revised this
chapter for the Fontana (1960) issue of* Miracles *in which Chapter
III is retitled 'The Cardinal Difficulty of Naturalism'.]*

A

In his reply Mr C. S. Lewis agreed that the words 'cause' and
'ground' were far from synonymous but said that the recognition
of a ground could be the cause of assent, and that assent was only
rational when such was its cause. He denied that such words as
'recognition' and 'perception' could be properly used of a mental
act among whose causes the thing perceived or recognized was
not one.

Miss Anscombe said that Mr Lewis had misunderstood her,
and thus the first part of the discussion was confined to the two
speakers who attempted to clarify their positions and their differences. Miss Anscombe said that Mr Lewis was still not distin-
guishing between 'having reasons' and 'having reasoned' in the
causal sense. Mr Lewis understood the speaker to be making a
tetrachotomy thus: (1) logical reasons; (2) having reasons (i.e.
psychological); (3) historical causes; (4) scientific causes or
observed regularities. The main point in his reply was that an
observed regularity was only the symptom of a cause, and not the
cause itself, and in reply to an interruption by the Secretary he
referred to his notion of cause as 'magical'. An open discussion
followed, in which some members tried to show Miss Anscombe
that there was a connection between ground and cause, while
others contended against the President [Lewis] that the test for

the validity of reason could never in any event be such a thing as the state of the blood stream. The President finally admitted that the word 'valid' was an unfortunate one. From the discussion in general it appeared that Mr Lewis would have to turn his argument into a rigorous analytic one, if his notion of 'validity' as the effect of causes were to stand the test of all the questions put to him.

B

I admit that *valid* was a bad word for what I meant; *veridical* (or *verific* or *veriferous*) would have been better. I also admit that the cause and effect relation between events and the ground and consequent relations between propositions are distinct. Since English uses the word *because* of both, let us here use *Because* CE for the cause and effect relation ('This doll always falls on its feet *because* CE its feet are weighted'), and *Because* GC for the ground and consequent relation ('A equals C *because* GC they both equal B'). But the sharper this distinction becomes the more my difficulty increases. If an argument is to be verific the conclusion must be related to the premises as consequent to ground, i.e. the conclusion is there *because* GC certain other propositions are true. On the other hand, our thinking the conclusion is an event and must be related to previous events as effect to cause, i.e. this act of thinking must occur *because* CE previous events have occurred. It would seem, therefore, that we never think the conclusion *because* GC it is the consequent of its grounds but only *because* CE certain previous events have happened. If so, it does not seem that the GC sequence makes us more likely to think the true conclusion than not. And this is very much what I meant by the difficulty in Naturalism.

15 Vivisection (1947)

It is the rarest thing in the world to hear a rational discussion of vivisection. Those who disapprove of it are commonly accused of 'sentimentality', and very often their arguments justify the accusation. They paint pictures of pretty little dogs on dissecting tables. But the other side lie open to exactly the same charge. They also often defend the practice by drawing pictures of suffering women and children whose pain can be relieved (we are assured) only by the fruits of vivisection. The one appeal, quite as clearly as the other, is addressed to emotion, to the particular emotion we call pity. And neither appeal proves anything. If the thing is right – and if right at all, it is a duty – then pity for the animal is one of the temptations we must resist in order to perform that duty. If the thing is wrong, then pity for human suffering is precisely the temptation which will most probably lure us into doing that wrong thing. But the real question – *whether* it is right or wrong – remains meanwhile just where it was.

A rational discussion of this subject begins by inquiring whether pain is, or is not, an evil. If it is not, then the case against vivisection falls. But then so does the case for vivisection. If it is not defended on the ground that it reduces human suffering, on what ground can it be defended? And if pain is not an evil, why should human suffering be reduced? We must therefore assume as a basis for the whole discussion that pain is an evil, otherwise there is nothing to be discussed.

Now if pain is an evil then the infliction of pain, considered in itself, must clearly be an evil act. But there are such things as

109

necessary evils. Some acts which would be bad, simply in themselves, may be excusable and even laudable when they are necessary means to a greater good. In saying that the infliction of pain, simply in itself, is bad, we are not saying that pain ought never to be inflicted. Most of us think that it can rightly be inflicted for a good purpose – as in dentistry or just and reformatory punishment. The point is that it always requires justification. On the man whom we find inflicting pain rests the burden of showing why an act which in itself would be simply bad is, in those particular circumstances, good. If we find a man giving pleasure it is for us to prove (if we criticize him) that his action is wrong. But if we find a man inflicting pain it is for him to prove that his action is right. If he cannot, he is a wicked man.

Now vivisection can only be defended by showing it to be right that one species should suffer in order that another species should be happier. And here we come to the parting of the ways. The Christian defender and the ordinary 'scientific' (i.e. naturalistic) defender of vivisection, have to take quite different lines.

The Christian defender, especially in the Latin countries, is very apt to say that we are entitled to do anything we please to animals because they 'have no souls'. But what does this mean? If it means that animals have no consciousness, then how is this known? They certainly behave as if they had, or at least the higher animals do. I myself am inclined to think that far fewer animals than is supposed have what we should recognize as consciousness. But that is only an opinion. Unless we know on other grounds that vivisection is right we must not take the moral risk of tormenting them on a mere opinion. On the other hand, the statement that they 'have no souls' may mean that they have no moral responsibilities and are not immortal. But the absence of 'soul' in that sense makes the infliction of pain upon them not easier but harder to justify. For it means that animals cannot deserve pain, nor profit morally by the discipline of pain, nor be recompensed by happiness in another life for suffering in this. Thus all the factors which render pain more tolerable or make it less totally evil in the case of human beings will be lacking in the beasts. 'Soullessness', in so far as it is relevant to the question at all, is an argument against vivisection.

The only rational line for the Christian vivisectionist to take is to say that the superiority of man over beast is a real objective fact, guaranteed by Revelation, and that the propriety of sacrificing beast to man is a logical consequence. We are 'worth more than many sparrows',[1] and in saying this we are not merely expressing a natural preference for our own species simply because it is our own but conforming to a hierarchical order created by God and really present in the universe whether any one acknowledges it or not. The position may not be satisfactory. We may fail to see how a benevolent Deity could wish us to draw such conclusions from the hierarchical order He has created. We may find it difficult to formulate a human right of tormenting beasts in terms which would not equally imply an angelic right of tormenting men. And we may feel that though objective superiority is rightly claimed for men, yet that very superiority ought partly to *consist in* not behaving like a vivisector: that we ought to prove ourselves better than the beasts precisely by the fact of acknowledging duties to them which they do not acknowledge to us. But on all these questions different opinions can be honestly held. If on grounds of our real, divinely ordained, superiority a Christian pathologist thinks it right to vivisect, and does so with scrupulous care to avoid the least dram or scruple of unnecessary pain, in a trembling awe at the responsibility which he assumes, and with a vivid sense of the high mode in which human life must be lived if it is to justify the sacrifices made for it, then

[1] Matthew 10:31.

(whether we agree with him or not) we can respect his point of view.

But of course the vast majority of vivisectors have no such theological background. They are most of them naturalistic and Darwinian. Now here, surely, we come up against a very alarming fact. The very same people who will most contemptuously brush aside any consideration of animal suffering if it stands in the way of 'research' will also, on another context, most vehemently deny that there is any radical difference between man and the other animals. On the naturalistic view the beasts are at bottom just the same *sort* of thing as ourselves. Man is simply the cleverest of the anthropoids. All the grounds on which a Christian might defend vivisection are thus cut from under our feet. We sacrifice other species to our own not because our own has any objective metaphysical privilege over others, but simply because it is ours. It may be very natural to have this loyalty to our own species, but let us hear no more from the naturalists about the 'sentimentality' of anti-vivisectionists. If loyalty to our own species, preference for man simply because we are men, is not a sentiment, then what is? It may be a good sentiment or a bad one. But a sentiment it certainly is. Try to base it on logic and see what happens!

But the most sinister thing about modern vivisection is this. If a mere sentiment justifies cruelty, why stop at a sentiment for the whole human race? There is also a sentiment for the white man against the black, for a *Herrenvolk* against the non-Aryans, for 'civilized' or 'progressive' peoples against 'savages' or 'backward' peoples. Finally, for our own country, party or class against others. Once the old Christian idea of a total difference in kind between man and beast has been abandoned, then no argument for experiments on animals can be found which is not also an argument for experiments on inferior men. If we cut up beasts simply because they cannot prevent us and because we are backing our own side in the struggle for existence, it is only logical to cut up imbeciles, criminals, enemies or capitalists for the same reasons. Indeed, experiments on men have already begun. We all hear that Nazi scientists have done them. We all suspect that our own scientists may begin to do so, in secret, at any moment.

The alarming thing is that the vivisectors have won the first round. In the nineteenth and eighteenth centuries a man was not stamped as a 'crank' for protesting against vivisection. Lewis Carroll protested, if I remember his famous letter correctly, on the very same ground which I have just used.[1] Dr Johnson – a man whose mind had as much *iron* in it as any man's – protested in a note on *Cymbeline* which is worth quoting in full. In Act I, scene v, the Queen explains to the Doctor that she wants poisons to experiment on 'such creatures as We count not worth the hanging – but none human'.[2] The Doctor replies:

> Your Highness
> Shall from this practice but make hard your heart.[3]

Johnson comments: 'The thought would probably have been more amplified, had our author lived to be shocked with such experiments as have been published in later times, by a race of men that have practised tortures without pity, and related them without shame, and are yet suffered to erect their heads among human beings.'[4]

The words are his, not mine, and in truth we hardly dare in

---

[1] 'Vivisection as a Sign of the Times', *The Works of Lewis Carroll*, ed. Roger Lancelyn Green (London, 1965), pp. 1089–92. See also 'Some Popular Fallacies about Vivisection', ibid., pp. 1092–1100.

[2] Shakespeare, *Cymbeline*, I, v, 19–20.

[3] ibid., 23.

[4] *Johnson on Shakespeare: Essays and Notes Selected and Set Forth with an Introduction by Sir Walter Raleigh* (London, 1908), p. 181.

these days to use such calmly stern language. The reason why we do not dare is that the other side has in fact won. And though cruelty even to beasts is an important matter, their victory is symptomatic of matters more important still. The victory of vivisection marks a great advance in the triumph of ruthless, non-moral utilitarianism over the old world of ethical law; a triumph in which we, as well as animals, are already the victims, and of which Dachau and Hiroshima mark the more recent achievements. In justifying cruelty to animals we put ourselves also on the animal level. We choose the jungle and must abide by our choice.

You will notice I have spent no time in discussing what actually goes on in the laboratories. We shall be told, of course, that there is surprisingly little cruelty. That is a question with which, at present, I have nothing to do. We must first decide what should be allowed: after that it is for the police to discover what is already being done.

16 Modern Translations of the Bible (1947)

It is possible that the reader who opens this volume[1] on the counter of a bookshop may ask himself why we need a new translation of any part of the Bible, and, if of any, why of the Epistles. 'Do we not already possess', it may be said, 'in the Authorized Version the most beautiful rendering which any language can boast?' Some people whom I have met go even further and feel that a modern translation is not only unnecessary but even offensive. They cannot bear to see the time-honoured words altered; it seems to them irreverent.

There are several answers to such people. In the first place the kind of objection which they feel to a new translation is very like the objection which was once felt to any English translation at all. Dozens of sincerely pious people in the sixteenth century shuddered at the idea of turning the time-honoured Latin of the Vulgate into our common and (as they thought) 'barbarous' English. A sacred truth seemed to them to have lost its sanctity when it was stripped of the polysyllabic Latin, long heard at Mass and at Hours, and put into 'language such as men do use' – language steeped in all the commonplace associations of the nursery, the inn, the stable and the street. The answer then was the same as the answer now. The only kind of sanctity which Scripture can lose (or at least New Testament Scripture) by being modernized

---

[1] This essay was originally published as an Introduction to J. B. Phillips' *Letters to Young Churches: A Translation of the New Testament Epistles* (London, 1947).

is an accidental kind which it never had for its writers or its earliest readers. The New Testament in the original Greek is not a work of literary art: it is not written in a solemn, ecclesiastical language, it is written in the sort of Greek which was spoken over the Eastern Mediterranean after Greek had become an international language and therefore lost its real beauty and subtlety. In it we see Greek used by people who have no real feeling for Greek words because Greek words are not the words they spoke when they were children. It is a sort of 'basic' Greek; a language without roots in the soil, a utilitarian, commercial and administrative language. Does this shock us? It ought not to, except as the Incarnation itself ought to shock us. The same divine humility which decreed that God should become a baby at a peasant-woman's breast, and later an arrested field-preacher in the hands of the Roman police, decreed also that He should be preached in a vulgar, prosaic and unliterary language. If you can stomach the one, you can stomach the other. The Incarnation is in that sense an irreverent doctrine: Christianity, in that sense, an incurably irreverent religion. When we expect that it should have come before the World in all the beauty that we now feel in the Authorized Version we are as wide of the mark as the Jews were in expecting that the Messiah would come as a great earthly King. The real sanctity, the real beauty and sublimity of the New Testament (as of Christ's life) are of a different sort: miles deeper or *further in*.

In the second place, the Authorized Version has ceased to be a good (that is, a clear) translation. It is no longer modern English: the meanings of words have changed. The same antique glamour which has made it (in the superficial sense) so 'beautiful', so 'sacred', so 'comforting', and so 'inspiring', has also made it in many places unintelligible. Thus where St Paul says 'I know nothing against myself', it translates 'I know nothing by myself'.[1]

---

[1] 1 Corinthians 4:4.

That was a good translation (though even then rather old-fashioned) in the sixteenth century: to the modern reader it means either nothing, or something quite different from what St Paul said. The truth is that if we are to have translation at all we must have periodical re-translation. There is no such thing as translating a book into another language once and for all, for a language is a changing thing. If your son is to have clothes it is no good buying him a suit once and for all: he will grow out of it and have to be re-clothed.

And finally, though it may seem a sour paradox – we must sometimes get away from the Authorized Version, if for no other reason, simply *because* it is so beautiful and so solemn. Beauty exalts, but beauty also lulls. Early associations endear but they also confuse. Through that beautiful solemnity the transporting or horrifying realities of which the book tells may come to us blunted and disarmed and we may only sigh with tranquil veneration when we ought to be burning with shame or struck dumb with terror or carried out of ourselves by ravishing hopes and adorations. Does the word 'scourged'[1] really come home to us like 'flogged'? Does 'mocked him'[2] sting like 'jeered at him'?

We ought therefore to welcome all new translations (when they are made by sound scholars) and most certainly those who are approaching the Bible for the first time will be wise not to begin with the Authorized Version – except perhaps for the historical books of the Old Testament where its archaisms suit the saga-like material well enough. Among modern translations those of Dr Moffatt[3] and Monsignor Knox[4] seem to me

---

[1] John 19:1.

[2] Matthew 27:29; Mark 15:20; Luke 22:63; 23:11, 36.

[3] James Moffatt (1870–1944), whose translation of the New Testament appeared in 1913, his translation of the Old Testament in 1924, the whole being revised in 1935.

[4] Ronald A. Knox (1888–1957) published a translation of the New Testament in 1945, and a translation of the Old Testament in 1949.

particularly good. The present volume concentrates on the Epistles and furnishes more help to the beginner: its scope is different. The preliminary abstracts to each letter will be found especially useful, and the reader who has not read the letters before might do well to begin by reading and reflecting on these abstracts at some length before he attempts to tackle the text. It would have saved me a great deal of labour if this book had come into my hands when I first seriously began to try to discover what Christianity was.

For a man who wants to make that discovery must face the Epistles. And whether we like it or not, most of them are by St Paul. He is the Christian author whom no one can by-pass.

A most astonishing misconception has long dominated the modern mind on the subject of St Paul. It is to this effect: that Jesus preached a kindly and simple religion (found in the Gospels) and that St Paul afterwards corrupted it into a cruel and complicated religion (found in the Epistles). This is really quite untenable. All the most terrifying texts come from the mouth of Our Lord: all the texts on which we can base such warrant as we have for hoping that all men will be saved come from St Paul. If it could be proved that St Paul altered the teaching of his Master in any way, he altered it in exactly the opposite way to that which is popularly supposed. But there is no real evidence for a pre-Pauline doctrine different from St Paul's. The Epistles are, for the most part, the earliest Christian documents we possess. The Gospels come later. They are not 'the Gospel', the statement of the Christian belief. They were written for those who had already been converted, who had already accepted 'the Gospel'. They leave out many of the 'complications' (that is, the theology) because they are intended for readers who have already been instructed in it. In that sense the Epistles are more primitive and more central than the Gospels – though not, of course, than the great events which the Gospels recount. God's act (the

Incarnation, the Crucifixion, and the Resurrection) comes first: the earliest theological analysis of it comes in the Epistles: then, when the generation who had known the Lord was dying out, the Gospels were composed to provide for believers a record of the great Act and of some of the Lord's sayings. The ordinary popular conception has put everything upside down. Nor is the cause far to seek. In the earlier history of every rebellion there is a stage at which you do not yet attack the King in person. You say, 'The King is all right. It is his Ministers who are wrong. They misrepresent him and corrupt all his plans – which, I'm sure, are good plans if only the Ministers would let them take effect.' And the first victory consists in beheading a few Ministers: only at a later stage do you go on and behead the King himself. In the same way, the nineteenth-century attack on St Paul was really only a stage in the revolt against Christ. Men were not ready in large numbers to attack Christ Himself. They made the normal first move – that of attacking one of His principal ministers. Everything they disliked in Christianity was therefore attributed to St Paul. It was unfortunate that their case could not impress anyone who had really read the Gospels and the Epistles with attention: but apparently few people had, and so the first victory was won. St Paul was impeached and banished and the world went on to the next step – the attack on the King Himself. But to those who wish to know what St Paul and his fellow-teachers really said the present volume will give great help.

17 On Living in an Atomic Age (1948)

In one way we think a great deal too much of the atomic bomb. 'How are we to live in an atomic age?' I am tempted to reply: 'Why, as you would have lived in the sixteenth century when the plague visited London almost every year, or as you would have lived in a Viking age when raiders from Scandinavia might land and cut your throat any night; or indeed, as you are already living in an age of cancer, an age of syphilis, an age of paralysis, an age of air raids, an age of railway accidents, an age of motor accidents.'

In other words, do not let us begin by exaggerating the novelty of our situation. Believe me, dear sir or madam, you and all whom you love were already sentenced to death before the atomic bomb was invented: and quite a high percentage of us were going to die in unpleasant ways. We had, indeed, one very great advantage over our ancestors – anaesthetics; but we have that still. It is perfectly ridiculous to go about whimpering and drawing long faces because the scientists have added one more chance of painful and premature death to a world which already bristled with such chances and in which death itself was not a chance at all, but a certainty.

This is the first point to be made: and the first action to be taken is to pull ourselves together. If we are all going to be destroyed by an atomic bomb, let that bomb when it comes find us doing sensible and human things – praying, working, teaching, reading, listening to music, bathing the children, playing tennis, chatting to our friends over a pint and a game of darts – not huddled together like frightened sheep and thinking about bombs. They may break our bodies (a microbe can do that) but they need not dominate our minds.

'But,' you reply, 'it is not death – not even painful and premature death – that we are bothering about. Of course the chance of *that* is not new. What is new is that the atomic bomb may finally and totally destroy civilization itself. The lights may be put out for ever.'

This brings us much nearer to the real point; but let me try to make clear exactly what I think that point is. What were your views about the ultimate future of civilization *before* the atomic bomb appeared on the scene? What did you think all this effort of humanity was to come to in the end? The real answer is known to almost everyone who has even a smattering of science; yet, oddly enough, it is hardly ever mentioned. And the real answer (almost beyond doubt) is that, with or without atomic bombs, the whole story is going to end in NOTHING. The astronomers hold out no hope that this planet is going to be permanently inhabitable. The physicists hold out no hope that organic life is going to be a permanent possibility in any part of the material universe. Not only this earth, but the whole show, all the suns of space, are to run down. Nature is a sinking ship. Bergson talks about the *élan vital*, and Mr Shaw talks about the 'Life-force' as if they could surge on for ever and ever. But that comes of concentrating on biology and ignoring the other sciences. There is really no such hope. Nature does not, in the long run, favour life. If Nature is all that exists – in other words, if there is no God and no life of some quite different sort somewhere outside Nature – then all stories will end in the same way: in a universe from which all life is banished without possibility of return. It will have been an accidental flicker, and there will be no one even to remember it. No doubt atomic bombs may cut its duration on this present planet shorter than it might have been; but the whole thing, even if it lasted for billions of years, must be so infinitesimally short in relation to the oceans of dead time which precede and follow it that I cannot feel excited about its curtailment.

What the wars and the weather (are we in for another of those periodic ice ages?) and the atomic bomb have really done is to remind us forcibly of the sort of world we are living in and which, during the prosperous period before 1914, we were beginning to forget. And this reminder is, so far as it goes, a good thing. We have been waked from a pretty dream, and now we can begin to talk about realities.

We see at once (when we have been waked) that the important question is not whether an atomic bomb is going to obliterate 'civilization'. The important question is whether 'Nature' – the thing studied by the sciences – is the only thing in existence. Because if you answer *yes* to the second question, then the first question only amounts to asking whether the inevitable frustration of all human activities may be hurried on by our own action instead of coming at its natural time. That is, of course, a question that concerns us very much. Even on a ship which will certainly sink sooner or later, the news that the boiler might blow up *now* would not be heard with indifference by anyone. But those who knew that the ship was sinking in any case would not, I think, be quite so desperately excited as those who had forgotten this fact, and were vaguely imagining that it might arrive somewhere.

It is, then, on the second question that we really need to make up our minds. And let us begin by supposing that Nature is all that exists. Let us suppose that nothing ever has existed or ever will exist except this meaningless play of atoms in space and time: that by a series of hundredth chances it has (regrettably) produced things like ourselves – conscious beings who now know that their own consciousness is an accidental result of the whole meaningless process and is therefore itself meaningless, though to us (alas!) it *feels* significant.

In this situation there are, I think, three things one might do:

(1) You might commit suicide. Nature which has (blindly, accidentally) given me for my torment this consciousness which demands meaning and value in a universe that offers neither, has luckily also given me the means of getting rid of it. I return the unwelcome gift. I will be fooled no longer.

(2) You might decide simply to have as good a time as possible. The universe is a universe of nonsense, but since you are here, grab what you can. Unfortunately, however, there is, on these terms, so very little left to grab – only the coarsest sensual pleasures. You can't, except in the lowest animal sense, be in love with a girl if you know (and keep on remembering) that all the beauties both of her person and of her character are a momentary and accidental pattern produced by the collision of atoms, and that your own response to them is only a sort of psychic phosphorescence arising from the behaviour of your genes. You can't go on getting any very serious pleasure from music if you know and remember that its air of significance is a pure illusion, that you like it only because your nervous system is irrationally conditioned to like it. You may still, in the lowest sense, have a 'good time'; but just in so far as it becomes very good, just in so far as it ever threatens to push you on from cold sensuality into real warmth and enthusiasm and joy, so far you will be forced to feel the hopeless disharmony between your own emotions and the universe in which you really live.

(3) You may defy the universe. You may say, 'Let it be irrational, I am not. Let it be merciless, I will have mercy. By whatever curious chance it has produced me, now that I am here I will live according to human values. I know the universe will win in the end, but what is that to me? I will go down fighting. Amid all this wastefulness I will persevere; amid all this competition, I will make sacrifices. Be damned to the universe!'

I suppose that most of us, in fact, while we remain materialists, adopt a more or less uneasy alternation between the second and the third attitude. And although the third is incomparably the better (it is, for instance, much more likely to 'preserve civilization'), both really shipwreck on the same rock. That rock – the disharmony between our own hearts and Nature – is obvious in the second. The third seems to avoid the rock by accepting disharmony from the outset and defying it. But it will not really work. In it, you hold up our own human standards against the idiocy of the universe. That is, we talk as if our own standards were something *outside* the universe which can be contrasted with it; as if we could judge the universe by some standard borrowed *from another source*. But if (as we were supposing) Nature – the space-time-matter system – is the only thing in existence, then of course there can be no other source for our standards. They must, like everything else, be the unintended and meaningless outcome of blind forces. Far from being a light from beyond Nature whereby Nature can be judged, they are only the way in which anthropoids of our species feel when the atoms under own own skulls get into certain states – those states being produced by causes quite irrational, unhuman, and non-moral. Thus the very ground on which we defy Nature crumbles under our feet. The standard we are applying is tainted at the source. If our standards are derived from this meaningless universe they must be as meaningless as it.

For most modern people, I think, thoughts of this kind have to be gone through before the opposite view can get a fair hearing. All Naturalism leads us to this in the end – to a quite final and hopeless discord between what our minds claim to be and what they really must be if Naturalism is true. They claim to be spirit; that is, to be reason, perceiving universal intellectual principles and universal moral laws and possessing free will. But if Naturalism is true they must in reality be merely arrangements of atoms in skulls, coming about by irrational causation. We never think a thought because it is true, only because blind Nature forces us to think it. We never do an act because it is right, only because blind Nature forces us to do it. It is when one has faced this preposterous conclusion that one is at last ready to listen to the voice that whispers: 'But suppose we really are spirits? Suppose we are not the offspring of Nature ...?'

For, really, the naturalistic conclusion is unbelievable. For one thing, it is only through trusting our own minds that we have come to know Nature herself. If Nature when fully known seems to teach us (that is, if the sciences teach us) that our own minds are chance arrangements of atoms, then there must have been some mistake; for if that were so, then the sciences themselves would be chance arrangements of atoms and we should have no reason for believing in them. There is only one way to avoid this deadlock. We must go back to a much earlier view. We must simply accept it that we are spirits, free and rational beings, at present inhabiting an irrational universe, and must draw the conclusion that we are *not derived from it*. We are strangers here. We come from somewhere else. Nature is not the only thing that exists. There is 'another world', and that is where we come from. And that explains why we do not feel at home here. A fish feels at home in the water. If we 'belonged here' we should feel at home here. All that we say about 'Nature red in tooth and claw', about death and time and mutability, all our half-amused, half-bashful attitude to our own bodies, is quite inexplicable on the theory that we are simply natural creatures. If this world is the only world, how did we come to find its laws either so dreadful or so comic? If there is no straight line elsewhere, how did we discover that Nature's line is crooked?

But what, then, is Nature, and how do we come to be imprisoned in a system so alien to us? Oddly enough, the question becomes much less sinister the moment one realizes that Nature is not all. Mistaken for our mother, she is terrifying and even abominable. But if she is only our sister – if she and we have a common Creator – if she is our sparring partner – then the situation is quite tolerable. Perhaps we are not here as prisoners but as colonists: only consider what we have done already to the dog, the horse, or the daffodil. She is indeed a rough playfellow. There are elements of evil in her. To explain that would carry us far back: I should have to speak of Powers and Principalities and all that would seem to a modern reader most mythological. This is not the place, nor do these questions come first. It is enough to say here that Nature, like us but in her different way, is much alienated from her Creator, though in her, as in us, gleams of the old beauty remain. But they are there not to be worshipped but to be enjoyed. She has nothing to teach us. It is our business to live by our own law not by hers: to follow, in private or in public life, the law of love and temperance even when they seem to be suicidal, and not the law of competition and grab, even when they seem to be necessary to our survival. For it is part of our spiritual law never to put survival first: not even the survival of our species. We must resolutely train ourselves to feel that the survival of Man on this Earth, much more of our own nation or culture or class, is not worth having unless it can be had by honourable and merciful means.

The sacrifice is not so great as it seems. Nothing is more likely to destroy a species or a nation than a determination to survive at all costs. Those who care for something else more than civilization are the only people by whom civilization is at all likely to be preserved. Those who want Heaven most have served Earth best. Those who love Man less than God do most for Man.

18 The Humanitarian Theory of Punishment
(1949)

In England we have lately had a controversy about Capital Punishment. I do not know whether a murderer is more likely to repent and make a good end on the gallows a few weeks after his trial or in the prison infirmary thirty years later. I do not know whether the fear of death is an indispensable deterrent. I need not, for the purpose of this article, decide whether it is a morally permissible deterrent. Those are questions which I propose to leave untouched. My subject is not Capital Punishment in particular, but that theory of punishment in general which the controversy showed to be almost universal among my fellow-countrymen. It may be called the Humanitarian theory. Those who hold it think that it is mild and merciful. In this I believe that they are seriously mistaken. I believe that the 'Humanity' which it claims is a dangerous illusion and disguises the possibility of cruelty and injustice without end. I urge a return to the traditional or Retributive theory not solely, not even primarily, in the interests of society, but in the interests of the criminal.

According to the Humanitarian theory, to punish a man because he deserves it, and as much as he deserves, is mere revenge, and, therefore, barbarous and immoral. It is maintained that the only legitimate motives for punishing are the desire to deter others by example or to mend the criminal. When this theory is combined, as frequently happens, with the belief that all crime is more or less pathological, the idea of mending tails off into that of healing or curing and punishment becomes therapeutic. Thus it appears at first sight that we have passed from the harsh and self-righteous notion of giving the wicked their deserts to the charitable and enlightened one of tending the psychologically sick. What could be more amiable? One little point which is taken for granted in this theory needs, however, to be made explicit. The things done to the criminal, even if they are called cures, will be just as compulsory as they were in the old days when we called them punishments. If a tendency to steal can be cured by psychotherapy, the thief will no doubt be forced to undergo the treatment. Otherwise, society cannot continue.

My contention is that this doctrine, merciful though it appears, really means that each one of us, from the moment he breaks the law, is deprived of the rights of a human being.

The reason is this. The Humanitarian theory removes from Punishment the concept of Desert. But the concept of Desert is the only connecting link between punishment and justice. It is only as deserved or undeserved that a sentence can be just or unjust. I do not here contend that the question 'Is it deserved?' is the only one we can reasonably ask about a punishment. We may very properly ask whether it is likely to deter others and to reform the criminal. But neither of these two last questions is a question about justice. There is no sense in talking about a 'just deterrent' or a 'just cure'. We demand of a deterrent not whether it is just but whether it will deter. We demand of a cure not whether it is just but whether it succeeds. Thus when we cease to consider what the criminal deserves and consider only what will cure him or deter others, we have tacitly removed him from the sphere of justice altogether; instead of a person, a subject of rights, we now have a mere object, a patient, a 'case'.

The distinction will become clearer if we ask who will be qualified to determine sentences when sentences are no longer held to derive their propriety from the criminal's deservings. On the old view the problem of fixing the right sentence was a moral problem. Accordingly, the judge who did it was a person trained in jurisprudence; trained, that is, in a science which deals with rights and duties, and which, in origin at least, was consciously accepting guidance from the Law of Nature, and from Scripture. We must admit that in the actual penal code of most countries at most times these high originals were so much modified by local custom, class interests, and utilitarian concessions, as to be very imperfectly recognizable. But the code was never in principle, and not always in fact, beyond the control of the conscience of the society. And when (say, in eighteenth-century England) actual punishments conflicted too violently with the moral sense of the community, juries refused to convict and reform was finally brought about. This was possible because, so long as we are thinking in terms of Desert, the propriety of the penal code, being a moral question, is a question on which every man has the right to an opinion, not because he follows this or that profession, but because he is simply a man, a rational animal enjoying the Natural Light. But all this is changed when we drop the concept of Desert. The only two questions we may now ask about a punishment are whether it deters and whether it cures. But these are not questions on which anyone is entitled to have an opinion simply because he is a man. He is not entitled to an opinion even if, in addition to being a man, he should happen also to be a jurist, a Christian, and a moral theologian. For they are not questions about principle but about matter of fact; and for such *cuiquam in sua arte credendum*.[1] Only the expert 'penologist' (let barbarous things have barbarous names), in the light of previous experiment, can tell us what is likely to deter: only the psychotherapist can tell us what is likely to cure. It will be in vain for the rest of us, speaking simply as men, to say, 'but this punishment is hideously unjust, hideously disproportionate to the criminal's deserts'. The experts with perfect logic will reply, 'But nobody was talking

---

[1] We must believe the expert in his own field.

about deserts. No one was talking about *punishment* in your archaic vindictive sense of the word. Here are the statistics proving that this treatment deters. Here are the statistics proving that this other treatment cures. What is your trouble?'

The Humanitarian theory, then, removes sentences from the hands of jurists whom the public conscience is entitled to criticize and places them in the hands of technical experts whose special sciences do not even employ such categories as rights or justice. It might be argued that since this transference results from an abandonment of the old idea of punishment, and, therefore, of all vindictive motives, it will be safe to leave our criminals in such hands. I will not pause to comment on the simple-minded view of fallen human nature which such a belief implies. Let us rather remember that the 'cure' of criminals is to be compulsory; and let us then watch how the theory actually works in the mind of the Humanitarian. The immediate starting point of this article was a letter I read in one of our Leftist weeklies. The author was pleading that a certain sin, now treated by our laws as a crime, should henceforward be treated as a disease. And he complained that under the present system the offender, after a term in gaol, was simply let out to return to his original environment where he would probably relapse. What he complained of was not the shutting up but the letting out. On his remedial view of punishment the offender should, of course, be detained until he was cured. And of course the official straighteners are the only people who can say when that is. The first result of the Humanitarian theory is, therefore, to substitute for a definite sentence (reflecting to some extent the community's moral judgement on the degree of ill-desert involved) an indefinite sentence terminable only by the word of those experts – and they are not experts in moral theology nor even in the Law of Nature – who inflict it. Which of us, if he stood in the dock, would not prefer to be tried by the old system?

It may be said that by the continued use of the word punishment and the use of the verb 'inflict' I am misrepresenting Humanitarians. They are not punishing, not inflicting, only healing. But do not let us be deceived by a name. To be taken without consent from my home and friends; to lose my liberty; to undergo all those assaults on my personality which modern psychotherapy knows how to deliver; to be re-made after some pattern of 'normality' hatched in a Viennese laboratory to which I never professed allegiance; to know that this process will never end until either my captors have succeeded or I have grown wise enough to cheat them with apparent success – who cares whether this is called Punishment or not? That it includes most of the elements for which any punishment is feared – shame, exile, bondage, and years eaten by the locust – is obvious. Only enormous ill-desert could justify it; but ill-desert is the very conception which the Humanitarian theory has thrown overboard.

If we turn from the curative to the deterrent justification of punishment we shall find the new theory even more alarming. When you punish a man *in terrorem*,[1] make of him an 'example' to others, you are admittedly using him as a means to an end; someone else's end. This, in itself, would be a very wicked thing to do. On the classical theory of Punishment it was of course justified on the ground that the man deserved it. That was assumed to be established before any question of 'making him an example' arose. You then, as the saying is, killed two birds with one stone; in the process of giving him what he deserved you set an example to others. But take away desert and the whole morality of the punishment disappears. Why, in Heaven's name, am I to be sacrificed to the good of society in this way? – unless, of course, I deserve it.

---

[1] To cause terror.

But that is not the worst. If the justification of exemplary punishment is not to be based on desert but solely on its efficacy as a deterrent, it is not absolutely necessary that the man we punish should even have committed the crime. The deterrent effect demands that the public should draw the moral, 'If we do such an act we shall suffer like that man.' The punishment of a man actually guilty whom the public think innocent will not have the desired effect; the punishment of a man actually innocent will, provided the public think him guilty. But every modern State has powers which make it easy to fake a trial. When a victim is urgently needed for exemplary purposes and a guilty victim cannot be found, all the purposes of deterrence will be equally served by the punishment (call it 'cure' if you prefer) of an innocent victim, provided that the public can be cheated into thinking him guilty. It is no use to ask me why I assume that our rulers will be so wicked. The punishment of an innocent, that is, an undeserving, man is wicked only if we grant the traditional view that righteous punishment means deserved punishment. Once we have abandoned that criterion, all punishments have to be justified, if at all, on other grounds that have nothing to do with desert. Where the punishment of the innocent can be justified on those grounds (and it could in some cases be justified as a deterrent) it will be no less moral than any other punishment. Any distaste for it on the part of a Humanitarian will be merely a hang-over from the Retributive theory.

It is, indeed, important to notice that my argument so far supposes no evil intentions on the part of the Humanitarian and considers only what is involved in the logic of his position. My contention is that good men (not bad men) consistently acting upon that position would act as cruelly and unjustly as the greatest tyrants. They might in some respects act even worse. Of all tyrannies a tyranny sincerely exercised for the good of its victims may be the most oppressive. It may be better to live under robber barons than under omnipotent moral busybodies. The robber baron's cruelty may sometimes sleep, his cupidity may at some point be satiated; but those who torment us for our own good will torment us without end for they do so with the approval of their own conscience. They may be more likely to go to Heaven yet at the same time likelier to make a Hell on earth. Their very kindness stings with intolerable insult. To be 'cured' against one's will and cured of states which we may not regard as disease is to be put on a level with those who have not yet reached the age of reason or those who never will; to be classed with infants, imbeciles, and domestic animals. But to be punished, however severely, because we have deserved it, because we 'ought to have known better', is to be treated as a human person made in God's image.

In reality, however, we must face the possibility of bad rulers armed with a Humanitarian theory of punishment. A great many popular blue-prints for a Christian society are merely what the Elizabethans called 'eggs in moonshine' because they assume that the whole society is Christian or that the Christians are in control. This is not so in most contemporary States. Even if it were, our rulers would still be fallen men, and, therefore, neither very wise nor very good. As it is, they will usually be unbelievers. And since wisdom and virtue are not the only or the commonest qualifications for a place in the government, they will not often be even the best unbelievers. The practical problem of Christian politics is not that of drawing up schemes for a Christian society, but that of living as innocently as we can with unbelieving fellow-subjects under unbelieving rulers who will never be perfectly wise and good and who will sometimes be very wicked and very foolish. And when they are wicked the Humanitarian theory of punishment will put in their hands a finer instrument of tyranny than wickedness ever had before. For if crime and disease are to be regarded as the same thing, it follows that any state of mind which our masters choose to call 'disease' can be treated as crime;

and compulsorily cured. It will be vain to plead that states of mind which displease government need not always involve moral turpitude and do not therefore always deserve forfeiture of liberty. For our masters will not be using the concepts of Desert and Punishment but those of disease and cure. We know that one school of psychology already regards religion as a neurosis. When this particular neurosis becomes inconvenient to government, what is to hinder government from proceeding to 'cure' it? Such 'cure' will, of course, be compulsory; but under the Humanitarian theory it will not be called by the shocking name of Persecution. No one will blame us for being Christian, no one will hate us, no one will revile us. The new Nero will approach us with the silky manners of a doctor, and though all will be in fact as compulsory as the *tunica molesta* or Smithfield or Tyburn, all will go on within the unemotional therapeutic sphere where words like 'right' and 'wrong' or 'freedom' and 'slavery' are never heard. And thus when the command is given, every prominent Christian in the land may vanish overnight into Institutions for the Treatment of the Ideologically Unsound, and it will rest with the expert gaolers to say when (if ever) they are to re-emerge. But it will not be persecution. Even if the treatment is painful, even if it is life-long, even if it is fatal, that will be only a regrettable accident; the intention was purely therapeutic. Even in ordinary medicine there were painful operations and fatal operations: so in this. But because they are 'treatment', not punishment, they can be criticized only by fellow-experts and on technical grounds, never by men as men and on grounds of justice.

This is why I think it essential to oppose the Humanitarian theory of punishment, root and branch, wherever we encounter it. It carries on its front a semblance of mercy which is wholly false. That is how it can deceive men of good will. The error began, perhaps, with Shelley's statement that the distinction between mercy and justice was invented in the courts of tyrants.

It sounds noble, and was indeed the error of a noble mind. But the distinction is essential. The older view was that mercy 'tempered' justice, or (on the highest level of all) that mercy and justice had met and kissed. The essential act of mercy was to pardon; and pardon in its very essence involves the recognition of guilt and ill-desert in the recipient. If crime is only a disease which needs cure, not sin which deserves punishment, it cannot be pardoned. How can you pardon a man for having a gumboil or a club foot? But the Humanitarian theory wants simply to abolish Justice and substitute Mercy for it. This means that you start being 'kind' to people before you have considered their rights, and then force upon them supposed kindnesses which no one but you will recognize as kindnesses and which the recipient will feel as abominable cruelties. You have overshot the mark. Mercy, detached from Justice, grows unmerciful. That is the important paradox. As there are plants which will flourish only in mountain soil, so it appears that Mercy will flower only when it grows in the crannies of the rock of Justice: transplanted to the Marshlands of mere Humanitarianism, it becomes a man-eating weed, all the more dangerous because it is still called by the same name as the mountain variety. But we ought long ago to have learned our lesson. We should be too old now to be deceived by those humane pretensions which have served to usher in every cruelty of the revolutionary period in which we live. These are the 'precious balms' which will 'break our heads'.[1]

There is a fine sentence in Bunyan: 'It came burning hot into my mind, whatever he said, and however he flattered, when he got me home to his House, he would sell me for a Slave.'[2] There is a fine couplet, too, in John Ball:

---

[1] Psalm 141:5.
[2] *The Pilgrim's Progress*, ed. James Blanton Wharey, second edition revised by Roger Sharrock, Oxford English Texts (Oxford, 1960), Part I, p. 70.

Be war or ye be wo;
Knoweth your freed from your foo.[1]

PART II

On Punishment: A Reply
by C. S. Lewis
(1954)

I have to thank the Editor for this opportunity of replying to two most interesting critiques of my article on the Humanitarian Theory of Punishment, one by Professor J. J. C. Smart[2] and the other by Drs N. Morris and D. Buckle.[3]

Professor Smart makes a distinction between questions of the First and of the Second Order. 'First' are questions like 'Ought I to return this book?'; 'Second', like 'Is promise-making a good institution?' He claims that these two Orders of question require different methods of treatment. The first can be answered by Intuition (in the sense which moral philosophers sometimes give that word). We 'see' what is 'right' at once, because the proposed action falls under a rule. But second-order questions can be answered only on 'utilitarian' principles. Since 'right' means 'agreeable to the rules' it is senseless to ask if the rules themselves are 'right'; we can only ask if they are useful. A parallel would be this: granted a fixed spelling we may ask whether a word is spelled correctly, but cannot ask whether the spelling system is correct, only if it is consistent or convenient. Or again,

---

[1] 'John Ball's Letter to the Peasants of Essex, 1381', lines 11–12, found in *Fourteenth Century Verse and Prose*, ed. Kenneth Sisam (Oxford, 1921), p. 161.
[2] 'Comment: The Humanitarian Theory of Punishment', *Res Judicatae*, Vol. VI (February 1954), pp. 368–71.
[3] 'Reply to C. S. Lewis', *Res Judicatae*, Vol. VI (June 1953), pp. 231–7.

a form may be grammatically right, but the grammar of a whole language cannot be right or wrong.

Professor Smart is here, of course, treating in a new way a very ancient distinction. It was realized by all the thinkers of the past that you could consider either (*a*) Whether an act was 'just' in the sense of conforming to a law or custom, or (*b*) Whether a law or custom was itself 'just'. To the ancient and medievals, however, the distinction was one between (*a*) Justice by law or convention, *nomo* (*i*) and (*b*) Justice 'simply' or 'by nature', *haplôs* or *physei*, or between (*a*) Positive Law, and (*b*) Natural Law. Both inquiries were about justice, but the distinction between them was acknowledged. The novelty of Professor Smart's system consists in confining the concept of justice to the first-order questions.

It is claimed that the new system (1) avoids a *petitio* inherent in any appeal to the Law of Nature or the 'simply' just; for 'to say that this is the Law of Nature is only to say that this is the rule we should adopt'; and (2) gets rid of dogmatic subjectivism. For the idea of desert in my article may be only 'Lewis's personal preference'.

I am not convinced, however, that Professor Smart's system does avoid these inconveniences.

Those rules are to be accepted which are useful to the community, utility being (I think) what will make that community 'happier'.[1] Does this mean that the happiness of the community is to be pursued *at all costs,* or only to be pursued in so far as this pursuit is compatible with certain degrees of mercy, human dignity and veracity? (I must not add 'of justice' because, in Professor Smart's view, the rules themselves cannot be either just or unjust.) If we take the second alternative, if we admit that there are some things, or even any one thing, which a community

---

[1] See the penultimate paragraph of Professor Smart's article.

ought not to do however much it will increase its happiness, then we have really given up the position. We are now judging the useful by some other standard (whether we call it Conscience, or Practical Reason, or Law of Nature or Personal Preference). Suppose then, we take the first alternative: the happiness of the community is to be pursued at all costs. In certain circumstances the costs may be very heavy. In war, in some not improbable future when the world's food runs short, during some threat of revolution, very shocking things may be likely to make the community happier or to preserve its existence. We cannot be sure that frame-ups, witch-hunts, even cannibalism, would never be in this sense 'useful'. Let us suppose (what, I am very sure, is false) that Professor Smart is prepared to go the whole hog. It then remains to ask him why he does so or why he thinks we should agree with him. He of all men cannot reply that *salus populi suprema lex*[1] is the Law of Nature; firstly, because we others know that 'the people should be preserved' is not the Law of Nature but only one clause in that Law. What then could a pursuit of the community's happiness at all costs be based on if not on Professor Smart's 'personal preference'? The real difference between him and me would then be simply that we have different desires. Or, rather, that I have one more desire than he. For, like him, I desire the continuance and happiness of my country (and species),[2] but then I also desire that they should be people of a certain sort, behaving in a certain way. The second desire is the stronger of the two. If I cannot have both, I had rather that the human race, having a certain quality in their lives, should

---

[1] The safety of the people is the highest law. Cicero, *De Legibus*, Book III, part iii, section 8.

[2] I am not sure whether for Professor Smart the 'community' means the nation or the species. If the former, difficulties arise about international morality, in discussing which I think Professor Smart would have to come to the species sooner or later.

continue for only a few centuries than that, losing freedom, friendship, dignity and mercy, and learning to be quite content without them, they should continue for millions of millennia. If it is merely a matter of wishes, there is really no further question for discussion. Lots of people feel like me, and lots feel the other way. I believe that it is in our age being decided which kind of men will win.

And that is why, if I may say so without discourtesy, Professor Smart and I both matter so little compared with Drs Morris and Buckle. We are only dons; they are criminologists, a lawyer and a psychiatrist respectively. And the only thing which leads me so far off my own beat as to write about 'Penology' at all is my intense anxiety as to which side in this immensely important conflict will have the Law for its ally. This leads me to the only serious disagreement between my two critics and myself.

Other disagreements there are, but they mainly turn on mis-understandings for which I am probably to blame. Thus:

(1) There was certainly too little, if there was anything, in my article about the protection of the community. I am afraid I took it for granted. But the distinction in my mind would not be, as my critics suppose [Morris and Buckle, p. 232], one between 'subsidiary' and 'vital' elements in punishment. I call the act of taking a packet of cigarettes off a counter and slipping it into one's pocket 'purchase' or 'theft' according as one does or does not pay for it. This does not mean that I consider the taking away of the goods as 'subsidiary' in an act of purchase. It means that what legitimizes it, what makes it purchase at all, is the paying. I call the sexual act chaste or unchaste according as the parties are or are not married to one another. This does not mean that I con-sider it as 'subsidiary' to marriage, but that what legitimizes it, what makes it a specimen of conjugal behaviour at all, is mar-riage. In the same way, I am ready to make both the protection of society and the 'cure' of the criminal as important as you please

in punishment, but only on a certain condition; namely, that the initial act of thus interfering with a man's liberty be justified on grounds of desert. Like payment in purchase, or marriage as regards the sexual act, it is this, and (I believe) this alone, which legitimizes our proceeding and makes it an instance of punishment at all, instead of an instance of tyranny – or, perhaps, of war.

(2) I agree about criminal *children* [see Morris and Buckle, p. 234]. There has been progress in this matter. Very primitive societies will 'try' and 'punish' an axe or a spear in cases of unintentional homicide. Somewhere (I think, in the Empire) during the later Middle Ages a pig was solemnly tried for murder. Till quite recently, we may (I don't know) have tried children as if they had adult responsibility. These things have rightly been abolished. But the whole question is whether you want the process to be carried further: whether you want us all to be simultaneously deprived of the protection and released from the responsibilities of adult citizenship and reduced to the level of the child, the pig and the axe. I don't want this because I don't think there are in fact any people who stand to the rest of us as adult to child, man to beast or animate to inanimate.[1] I think the laws which laid down a 'desertless' theory of punishment would in reality be made and administered by people just like the rest of us.

But the real disagreement is this. Drs Morris and Buckle, fully alive to dangers of the sort I dread and reprobating them no less than I, believe that we have a safeguard. It lies in the Courts, in their incorruptible judges, their excellent techniques and 'the controls of natural justice which the law has built up' [p. 233]. Yes; if the whole tradition of natural justice which the law has for

---

[1] This is really the same objection as that which I would make to Aristotle's theory of slavery *(Politics* 1254A *et seq.).* We can all recognize the 'natural' slaves (I am perhaps one myself) but where are the 'natural' masters?

so long incorporated, will survive the completion of that change in our attitude to punishment which we are now discussing. But that for me is precisely the question. Our Courts, I agree, 'have traditionally represented the common man and the common man's view of morality' [p. 233]. It is true that we must extend the term 'common man' to cover Locke, Grotius, Hooker, Poynet, Aquinas, Justinian, the Stoics and Aristotle, but I have no objection to that; in one most important, and to me glorious, sense they were all common men.[1] But that whole tradition is tied up with ideas of free will, responsibility, rights and the law of nature. Can it survive in Courts whose penal practice daily subordinates 'desert' to therapy and the protection of society? Can the Law assume one philosophy in practice and continue to enjoy the safeguards of a different philosophy?

I write as the son of one lawyer and the life-long friend of another, to two criminologists one of whom is a lawyer. I believe an approximation between their view and mine is not to be despaired of, for we have the same ends at heart. I wish society to be protected and I should be very glad if all punishments were also cures. All I plead for is the *prior* condition of ill-desert; loss of liberty justified on retributive grounds *before* we begin considering the other factors. After that, as you please. Till that, there is really no question of 'punishment'. We are not such poltroons that we want to be protected unconditionally, though when a man has deserved punishment we shall very properly look to our protection in devising it. We are not such busybodies that we want to improve all our neighbours by force; but when one of our neighbours has justly forfeited his right not to be interfered with, we shall charitably try to make his punishment improve him. But we will not presume to teach him (who, after all, are

---

[1] See also Lewis: *The Abolition of Man* (London, 1943), especially the Appendix.

we?) till he has merited that we should 'larn him'. Will Dr Morris and Dr Buckle come so far to meet me as that? On their decision and on that of others in similar important offices, depends, I believe, the continued dignity and beneficence of that great discipline the Law, but also much more. For, if I am not deceived, we are all at this moment helping to decide whether humanity shall retain all that has hitherto made humanity worth preserving, or whether we must slide down into the sub-humanity imagined by Mr Aldous Huxley and George Orwell and partially realized in Hitler's Germany. For the extermination of the Jews really would have been 'useful' if the racial theories had been correct; there is no foretelling what may come to seem, or even to be, 'useful', and 'necessity' was always 'the tyrant's plea'.

19 The Pains of Animals (1950)
A Problem in Theology[1]

The Inquiry by C. E. M. Joad

For many years the problem of pain and evil seemed to me to offer an insuperable objection to Christianity. Either God could abolish them but did not, in which case, since He deliberately tolerated the presence in the universe of a state of affairs which was bad, I did not see how He could be good; or He wanted to abolish them but could not, in which case I did not see how He could be all-powerful. The dilemma is as old as St Augustine, and nobody pretends that there is an easy way of escape.

Moreover, all the attempts to explain pain away, or to mitigate its stark ferocity, or to present it as other than a very great evil, perhaps the greatest of evils, are palpable failures. They are testimonies to the kindness of men's hearts or perhaps to the quea- siness of their consciences, rather than to the sharpness of their wits.

And yet, granting pain to be an evil, perhaps the greatest of evils, I have come to accept the Christian view of pain as not incompatible with the Christian concept of the Creator and of

[1] In his book, *The Problem of Pain*, one of the questions Lewis addressed himself to was how to account for the occurrence of pain in a universe which is the creation of an all-good God, and in creatures who are not morally sinful. His chapter on 'Animal Pain' provoked a counter-inquiry from the late C. E. M. Joad, who was Head of the Department of Philosophy in the University of London. The result was this controversy, first published in *The Month*.

the world that He has made. That view I take to be briefly as follows: It was of no interest to God to create a species consisting of virtuous automata, for the 'virtue' of automata who can do no other than they do is a courtesy title only; it is analogous to the 'virtue' of the stone that rolls downhill or of the water that freezes at 32°. To what end, it may be asked, should God create such creatures? That He might be praised by them? But automatic praise is a mere succession of noises. That He might love them? But they are essentially unlovable; you cannot love puppets. And so God gave man free will that he might increase in virtue by his own efforts and become, as a free moral being, a worthy object of God's love. Freedom entails freedom to go wrong: man did, in fact, go wrong, misusing God's gift and doing evil. Pain is a by-product of evil; and so pain came into the world as a result of man's misuse of God's gift of free will.

So much I can understand; so much, indeed, I accept. It is plausible; it is rational; it hangs together.

But now I come to a difficulty, to which I see no solution; indeed, it is in the hope of learning of one that this article is written. This is the difficulty of animal pain, and, more particularly, of the pain of the animal world before man appeared upon the cosmic scene. What account do theologians give of it? The most elaborate and careful account known to me is that of C. S. Lewis.

He begins by making a distinction between sentience and consciousness. When we have the sensations *a*, *b* and *c*, the fact that we have them and the fact that we know that we have them imply that there is something which stands sufficiently outside them to notice that they occur and that they succeed one another. This is consciousness, the consciousness to which the sensations happen. In other words, the experience of succession, the succession of sensations, demands a self or soul which is other than the sensations which it experiences. (Mr Lewis invokes the helpful metaphor of the bed of a river along which the stream of sensations flows.) Consciousness, therefore, implies a continuing *ego* which recognizes the succession of sensations; sentience is their mere succession. Now animals have sentience but not consciousness. Mr Lewis illustrates as follows:

> This would mean that if you give such a creature two blows with a whip, there are, indeed, two pains: but there is no co-ordinating self which can recognize that 'I have had two pains'. Even in the single pain there is no self to say 'I am in pain' — for if it could distinguish itself from the sensation — the bed from the stream — sufficiently to say 'I am in pain', it would also be able to connect the two sensations as *its* experience.[1]

(*a*) I take Mr Lewis's point — or, rather, I take it without perceiving its relevance. The question is how to account for the occurrence of pain (i) in a universe which is the creation of an all-good God; (ii) in creatures who are not morally sinful. To be told that the creatures are not really creatures, since they are not conscious in the sense of consciousness defined, does not really help matters. If it be true, as Mr Lewis says, that the right way to put the matter is not 'This animal is feeling pain' but 'Pain is taking place in this animal',[2] pain is nevertheless taking place. Pain is felt even if there is no continuing *ego* to feel it and to relate it to past and to future pains. Now it is the fact that pain is felt, no matter who or what feels it, or whether any continuing consciousness feels it, in a universe planned by a good God, that demands explanation.

(*b*) Secondly, the theory of sentience as mere succession of sensations presupposes that there is no continuing consciousness. No continuing consciousness presupposes no memory. It

---

[1] *The Problem of Pain* (London, 1940), ch. 9, p. 120.
[2] ibid., pp. 120–1.

seems to me to be nonsense to say that animals do not remember. The dog who cringes at the sight of the whip by which he has been constantly beaten *behaves* as if he remembers, and behaviour is all that we have to go by. In general, we all act upon the assumption that the horse, the cat, and the dog with which we are acquainted remember very well, remember sometimes better than we do. Now I do not see how it is possible to explain the fact of memory without a continuing consciousness.

Mr Lewis recognizes this and concedes that the higher animals – apes, elephants, dogs, cats and so on – have a self which connects experiences; have, in fact, what he calls a soul.[1] But this assumption presents us with a new set of difficulties.

(a) If animals have souls, what is to be done about their immortality? The question, it will be remembered, is elaborately debated in Heaven at the beginning of Anatole France's *Penguin Island* after the short-sighted St Mael has baptized the penguins, but no satisfactory solution is offered.

(b) Mr Lewis suggests that the higher domestic animals achieve immortality as members of a corporate society of which the head is man. It is, apparently, 'The-goodman-and-the-goodwife-ruling-their-children-and-their-beasts-in-the-good-homestead'[2] who survive. 'If you ask,' he writes, 'concerning an animal thus raised as a member of the whole Body of the homestead, where its personal identity resides, I answer, 'Where its identity always did reside even in the earthly life – in its relation to the Body and, specially, to the master who is the head of that Body.' In other words, the man will know his dog: the dog will know its master and, in knowing him, will *be* itself.'[3]

Whether this is good theology, I do not know, but to our present inquiry it raises two difficulties.

[1] ibid., p. 121.
[2] ibid., p. 127.
[3] ibid., p. 128.

(i) It does not cover the case of the higher animals who do not know man – for example, apes and elephants – but who are yet considered by Mr Lewis to have souls.

(ii) If one animal may attain good immortal selfhood in and through a good man, he may attain bad immortal selfhood in and through a bad man. One thinks of the overnourished lapdogs of idle overnourished women. It is a little hard that when, through no fault of their own, animals fall to selfish, self-indulgent, or cruel masters, they should through eternity form part of selfish, self-indulgent, or cruel superpersonal wholes and perhaps be punished for their participation in them.

(c) If the animals have souls and, presumably, freedom, the same sort of explanation must be adopted for pain in animals as is offered for pain in men. Pain, in other words, is one of the evils consequent upon sin. The higher animals, then, are corrupt. The question arises, who corrupted them? There seem to be two possible answers: (1) The Devil; (2) Man.

(1) Mr Lewis considers this answer. The animals, he says, may originally all have been herbivorous. They became carnivorous – that is to say, they began to prey upon, to tear, and to eat one another – because 'some mighty created power had already been at work for ill on the material universe, or the solar system, or, at least, the planet Earth, before ever man came on the scene ... If there is such a power ... it may well have corrupted the animal creation before man appeared.'[1]

I have three comments to make:

(i) I find the supposition of Satan tempting monkeys frankly incredible. This, I am well aware, is not a logical objection. It is one's imagination – or perhaps one's common sense? – that revolts against it.

[1] ibid., pp. 122–3.

(ii) Although most animals fall victims to the redness of nature's 'tooth and claw', many do not. The sheep falls down the ravine, breaks its leg, and starves; hundreds of thousands of migrating birds die every year of hunger; creatures are struck and not killed by lightning, and their seared bodies take long to die. Are these pains due to corruption?

(iii) The case of animals without souls cannot, on Mr Lewis's own showing, be brought under the 'moral corruption' explanation. Yet consider just one instance of nature's arrangements. The wasps, *Ichneumonidae,* sting their caterpillar prey in such a way as to paralyse its nerve centres. They then lay their eggs on the helpless caterpillar. When the grubs hatch from the eggs, they immediately proceed to feed upon the living but helpless flesh of their incubators, the paralysed but still sentient caterpillars.

It is hard to suppose that the caterpillar feels no pain when slowly consumed; harder still to ascribe the pain to moral corruption; hardest of all to conceive how such an arrangement could have been planned by an all-good and all-wise Creator.

(2) The hypothesis that the animals were corrupted by man does not account for animal pain during the hundreds of millions of years (probably about 900 million) when the earth contained living creatures but did not contain man.

In sum, either animals have souls or they have no souls. If they have none, pain is felt for which there can be no moral responsibility, and for which no misuse of God's gift of moral freedom can be invoked as an excuse. If they have souls, we can give no plausible account (*a*) of their immortality – how draw the line between animals with souls and men with souls? – or (*b*) of their moral corruption, which would enable Christian apologists to place them in respect of their pain under the same heading of explanation as that which is proposed and which I am prepared to accept for man.

The Pains of Animals (1950)

It may well be that there is an answer to this problem. I would be grateful to anyone who would tell me what it is.

The Reply by C. S. Lewis

Though there is pleasure as well as danger in encountering so sincere and economical a disputant as Dr Joad, I do so with no little reluctance. Dr Joad writes not merely as a controversialist who demands, but as an inquirer who really desires, an answer. I come into the matter at all only because my answers have already failed to satisfy him. And it is embarrassing to me, and possibly depressing to him, that he should, in a manner, be sent back to the same shop which has once failed to supply the goods. If it were wholly a question of defending the original goods, I think I would let it alone. But it is not exactly that. I think he has perhaps slightly misunderstood what I was offering for sale.

Dr Joad is concerned with the ninth chapter of my *Problem of Pain*. And the first point I want to make is that no one would gather from his article how confessedly speculative that chapter was. This was acknowledged in my preface and repeatedly emphasized in the chapter itself. This, of course, can bring no ease to Dr Joad's difficulties; unsatisfactory answers do not become satisfactory by being tentative. I mention the character of the chapter to underline the fact that it stands on a rather different level from those which preceded it. And that difference suggests the place which my 'guess-work' about Beasts (so I called it at the time and call it still) had in my own thought, and which I would like this whole question to have in Dr Joad's thought too.

The first eight chapters of my book attempted to meet the *prima facie* case against Theism based on human pain. They were the fruit of a slow change of mind not at all unlike that which Dr Joad himself has undergone and to which, when it had been completed, he at once bore honourable and (I expect) costly witness. The process of his thought differed at many points (very likely for the better) from the process of mine. But we came out, more or less, at the same place. The position of which he says in his article 'So much I understand; so much, indeed, I accept' is very close to that which I reached in the first eight chapters of my *Problem*.

So far, so good. Having 'got over' the problem of human pain, Dr Joad and I both find ourselves faced with the problem of animal pain. We do not at once part company even then. We both (if I read him correctly) turn with distaste from 'the easy speeches that comfort cruel men',[1] from theologians who do not seem to see that there is a real problem, who are content to say that animals are, after all, only animals. To us, pain without guilt or moral fruit, however low and contemptible the sufferer may be, is a very serious matter.

I now ask Dr Joad to observe rather closely what I do at this point, for I doubt if it is exactly what he thinks. I do not advance a doctrine of animal sentience as proved and thence conclude. 'Therefore beasts are not sacrificed without recompense, and therefore God is just.' If he will look carefully at my ninth chapter he will see that it can be divided into two very unequal parts: Part One consisting of the first paragraph, and Part Two of all the rest. They might be summarized as follows:

Part One. The data which God has given us enable us in some degree to understand human pain. We lack such data about beasts. We know neither what they are nor why they are. All that we can say for certain is that if God is good (and I think we have grounds for saying that He is) then the appearance of divine

---

[1] G. K. Chesterton, 'A Hymn', line 11. The first line begins 'O God of earth and altar'.

cruelty in the animal world must be a false appearance. What the reality behind the false appearance may be we can only guess.

Part Two. And here are some of my own guesses.

Now it matters far more whether Dr Joad agrees with Part One than whether he approves any of the speculations in Part Two. But I will first deal, so far as I can, with his critique of the speculations.

(1) Conceding *(positionis causa)*[1] my distinction between sentience and consciousness, Dr Joad thinks it irrelevant. 'Pain is felt', he writes, 'even if there is no continuing *ego* to feel it and to relate it to past and future pain', and 'it is the fact that pain is felt, no matter who or what feels it … that demands explanation.' I agree that in one sense it does not (for the present purpose) matter 'who or what' feels it. That is, it does not matter how humble, or helpless, or small, or how removed from our spontaneous sympathies, the sufferer is. But it surely does matter how far the sufferer is capable of what we can recognize as misery, how far the genuinely pitiable is consistent with its mode of existence. It will hardly be denied that the more coherently conscious the subject is, the more pity and indignation its pains deserve. And this seems to me to imply that the less coherently conscious, the less they deserve. I still think it possible for there to be a pain so instantaneous (through the absence of all perception of succession) that its 'unvalue', if I may coin the word, is indistinguishable from zero. A correspondent has instanced shooting pains in our own experience on those occasions when they are unaccompanied by fear. They may be intense: but they are gone as we recognize their intensity. In my own case I do not find anything in them which demands pity; they are, rather, comical. One tends to laugh. A series of such pains is, no doubt,

[1] for the sake of argument.

terrible; but then the contention is that the series could not exist for sentience without consciousness.

(2) I do not think that behaviour 'as if from memory' proves memory in the conscious sense. A non-human observer might suppose that if we blink our eyes at the approach of an object we are 'remembering' pains received on previous occasions. But no memories, in the full sense, are involved. (It is, of course, true that the behaviour of the organism is modified by past experiences, and we may thus by metonymy say that the nerves remember what the mind forgets; but that is not what Dr Joad and I are talking of.) If we are to suppose memory in all cases where behaviour adapts itself to a probable recurrence of past events, shall we not have to assume in some insects an inherited memory of their parents' breeding habits? And are we prepared to believe this?

(3) Of course my suggested theory of the tame animals' resurrection 'in' its human (and therefore, indirectly, divine) context does not cover wild animals or ill-treated tame ones. I had made the point myself, and added 'it is intended only as an illustration ... of the general principles to be observed in framing a theory of animal resurrection'.[1] I went on to make an alternative suggestion, observing, I hope, the same principles. My chief purpose at this stage was at once to liberate imagination and to confirm a due agnosticism about the meaning and destiny of brutes. I had begun by saying that if our previous assertion of divine goodness was sound, we might be sure that *in some way or other* 'all would be well, and all manner of thing would be well'.[2] I wanted to reinforce this by indicating how little we knew and, therefore, how many things one might keep in mind as possibilities.

---

[1] *The Problem of Pain*, p. 128.
[2] Lady Julian of Norwich, *Sixteenth Revelations of Divine Love*, ch. 29.

(4) If Dr Joad thinks I pictured Satan 'tempting monkeys', I am myself to blame for using the word 'encouraged'. I apologize for the ambiguity. In fact, I had not supposed that 'temptation' (that is, solicitation of the will) was the only mode in which the Devil could corrupt or impair. It is probably not the only mode in which he can impair even human beings; when Our Lord spoke of the deformed woman as one 'bound by Satan',[1] I presume He did not mean that she had been tempted into deformity. Moral corruption is not the only kind of corruption. But the word *corruption* was perhaps ill-chosen and invited misunderstanding. *Distortion* would have been safer.

(5) My correspondent writes 'that even the severest injuries in most invertebrate animals are almost if not quite painless is the view of most biologists. Loeb collected much evidence to show that animals without cerebral hemispheres were indistinguishable from plants in every psychological respect. The instance readily occurs of the caterpillars which serenely go on eating though their interiors are being devoured by the larvae of some ichneumon fly. The Vivisection Act does not apply to invertebrates; which indicates the views of those who framed it.'

(6) Though Dr Joad does not raise the point, I cannot forbear adding some most interesting suggestions about animal fear from the same correspondent. He points out that human fear contains two elements: (*a*) the physical sensations, due to the secretions, etc.; (*b*) the mental images of what will happen if one loses hold, or if the bomb falls here, or if the train leaves the rails. Now (*a*), in itself, is so far from being an unmixed grief, that when we can get it without (*b*), or with unbelieved (*b*), or even with subdued (*b*), vast numbers of people like it: hence switchbacks, water-shoots, fast motoring, mountain climbing.

---

[1] Luke 13:16.

But all this is nothing to a reader who does not accept Part One in my ninth chapter. No man in his senses is going to start building up a theodicy with speculations about the minds of beasts as his foundation. Such speculations are in place only, as I said, to open the imagination to possibilities and to deepen and confirm our inevitable agnosticism about the reality, and only after the ways of God *to Man* have ceased to seem unjustifiable. We do not know the answer: these speculations were guesses at what it might possibly be. What really matters is the argument that there must be an answer: the argument that if, in our own lives, where alone (if at all) we know Him, we come to recognize the *pulchritudo tam antiqua et tam nova*,[1] then, in other realms where we cannot know Him *(connaître)*, though we may know *(savoir)* some few things about Him – then, despite appearances to the contrary, He cannot be a power of darkness. For there were appearances to the contrary in our own realm too; yet, for Dr Joad as for me, they have somehow been got over.

I know that there are moments when the incessant continuity and desperate helplessness of what at least seems to be animal suffering makes every argument for Theism sound hollow, and when (in particular) the insect world appears to be Hell itself visibly in operation around us. Then the old indignation, the old pity arises. But how strangely ambivalent this experience is: I need not expound the ambivalence at much length, for I think I have done so elsewhere, and I am sure that Dr Joad had long discerned it for himself. If I regard this pity and indignation simply as subjective experiences of my own with no validity beyond their strength at the moment (which next moment will change), I can hardly use them as standards whereby to arraign the creation. On the contrary, they become strong as arguments against God just in so far as I take them to be transcendent illuminations

[1] Beauty so ancient and so new, St Augustine, Confessions, Bk. X, ch. 27.

to which creation must conform or be condemned. They are arguments against God only if they are themselves the voice of God. The more Shelleyan, the more Promethean my revolt, the more surely it claims a divine sanction. That the mere contingent Joad or Lewis, born in an era of secure and liberal civilization and imbibing from it certain humanitarian sentiments, should happen to be offended by suffering – what is that to the purpose? How will one base an argument for or against God on such an historical accident?

No. Not in so far as we feel these things, but in so far as we claim to be right in feeling them, in so far as we are sure that these standards have an empire *de jure* over all possible worlds, so far, and so far only, do they become a ground for disbelief – and at the same moment, for belief. God within us steals back at the moment of our condemning the apparent God without. Thus in Tennyson's poem the man who had become convinced that the God of his inherited creed was evil exclaimed: 'If there be such a God, may the Great God curse him and bring him to nought.'[1] For if there is no 'Great God' behind the curse who curses? Only a puppet of the little apparent 'God'. His very curse is poisoned at the root: it is just the same sort of event as the very cruelties he is condemning, part of the meaningless tragedy.

From this I see only two exits: either that there is a Great God, and also a 'God of this world',[2] a prince of the powers of the air, whom the Great God does curse, and sometimes curse through us; or else that the operations of the Great God are not what they seem to me to be.

---

[1] 'Despair', 19, 106.
[2] 2 Corinthians 4:4.

20 Is Theism Important?[1] (1952)

I have lost the notes of what I originally said in replying to Professor Price's paper and cannot now remember what it was, except that I welcomed most cordially his sympathy with the Polytheists. I still do. When grave persons express their fear that England is relapsing into Paganism, I am tempted to reply, 'Would that she were!' For I do not think it at all likely that we shall ever see Parliament opened by the slaughtering of a garlanded white bull in the House of Lords, or Cabinet Ministers leaving sandwiches in Hyde Park as an offering for the Dryads. If such a state of affairs came about, then the Christian apologist would have something to work on. For a Pagan, as history shows, is a man eminently convertible to Christianity. He is essentially, the pre-Christian, or sub-Christian, religious man. The post-Christian man of our own day differs from him as much as a *divorcée* differs from a virgin. The Christian and the Pagan have much more in common with one another than either has with the writers of the *New Statesman*; and those writers would of course agree with me. For the rest, what now occurs to me after re-reading Professor Price's paper is something like this.

[1] This is a reply to a paper Professor H. H. Price read to the Oxford Socratic Club. Professor Price's paper was published under the same title in *The Socratic Digest*, No. 5 (1952), pp. 39–47, and Lewis's answer, printed here, was originally published in the same periodical.

Is Theism Important? (1952)

1. I think we must introduce into the discussion a distinction between two senses of the word *Faith*. This may mean (*a*) a settled intellectual assent. In that sense faith (or 'belief') in God hardly differs from faith in the uniformity of nature or in the consciousness of other people. This is what, I think, has sometimes been called a 'notional' or 'intellectual' or 'carnal' faith. It may also mean (*b*) a trust, or confidence, in the God whose existence is thus assented to. This involves an attitude of the will. It is more like our confidence in a friend. It would be generally agreed that Faith in sense A is not a religious state. The devils who 'believe and tremble'[1] have Faith-A. A man who curses or ignores God may have Faith-A. Philosophical arguments for the existence of God are presumably intended to produce Faith-A. No doubt those who construct them are anxious to produce Faith-A because it is a necessary precondition of Faith-B, and in that sense their ultimate intention is religious. But their immediate object, the conclusion they attempt to prove, is not. I therefore think they cannot be justly accused of trying to get a religious conclusion out of non-religious premises. I agree with Professor Price that this cannot be done: but I deny that the religious philosophers are trying to do it.

I also think that in some ages, what claim to be Proofs of Theism have had much more efficacy in producing Faith-A than Professor Price suggests. Nearly everyone I know who has embraced Christianity in adult life has been influenced by what seemed to him to be at least probable arguments for Theism. I have known some who were completely convinced by Descartes' Ontological Proof:[2] that is, they received Faith-A from Descartes first and then went on to seek, and to find, Faith-B. Even quite

---

[1] James 2:19.
[2] This is briefly summed up in René Descartes' *Discours de la Méthode*, Part iv, in which he says 'I think, therefore I am'.

uneducated people who have been Christians all their lives not infrequently appeal to some simplified form of the Argument from Design. Even acceptance of tradition implies an argument which sometimes becomes explicit in the form 'I reckon all those wise men wouldn't have believed in it if it weren't true.'

Of course Faith-A usually involves a degree of subjective certitude which goes beyond the logical certainty, or even the supposed logical certainty, of the arguments employed. It may retain this certitude for a long time, I expect, even without the support of Faith-B. This excess of certitude in a settled assent is not at all uncommon. Most of those who believe in Uniformity of Nature, Evolution, or the Solar System, share it.

2. I doubt whether religious people have ever supposed that Faith-B follows automatically on the acquisition of Faith-A. It is described as a 'gift'.[1] As soon as we have Faith-A in the existence of God, we are instructed to ask from God Himself the gift of Faith-B. An odd request, you may say, to address to a First Cause, an *Ens Realissimum*, or an *Unmoved Mover*. It might be argued, and I think I would argue myself, that even such an aridly philosophical God rather fails to invite than actually repels a personal approach. It would, at any rate, do no harm to try it. But I fully admit that most of those who, having reached Faith-A, pray for Faith-B, do so because they have already had something like religious experience. Perhaps the best way of putting it would be to say that Faith-A converts into religious experience what was hitherto only potentially or implicitly religious. In this modified form I would accept Professor Price's view that philosophical proofs never, by themselves, lead to religion. Something at least *quasi*-religious uses them before, and the 'proofs' remove

---

[1] e.g. 1 Corinthians 12:1–11; Ephesians 2:8.

an inhibition which was preventing their development into religion proper.

This is not exactly *fides quaerens intellectum*,[1] for these quasi-religious experiences were not *fides*. In spite of Professor Price's rejection I still think Otto's account of the Numinous[2] is the best analysis of them we have. I believe it is a mistake to regard the Numinous as merely an affair of 'feeling'. Admittedly, Otto can describe it only by referring to the emotions it arouses in us; but then nothing can be described except in terms of its effects in consciousness. We have in English an exact name for the emotion aroused by the Numinous, which Otto, writing in German, lacked; we have the word Awe — an emotion very like fear, with the important difference that it need imply no estimate of danger. When we fear a tiger, we fear that it may kill us: when we fear a ghost — well, we just fear the ghost, not this or that mischief which it may do us. The Numinous or Awful is that of which we have this, as it were, objectless or disinterested fear — this awe. And 'the Numinous' is not a name for our own feeling of Awe any more than 'the Contemptible' is a name for contempt. It is the answer to the question 'Of what do you feel awe?' And what we feel awe of is certainly not itself awe.

With Otto and, in a sense, with Professor Price, I would find the seed of religious experience in our experience of the Numinous. In an age like our own such experience does occur but, until religion comes and retrospectively transforms it, it usually appears to the subject to be a special form of aesthetic experience. In ancient times I think experience of the Numinous developed into the Holy only in so far as the Numinous (not in itself at all necessarily moral) came to be connected with the morally good. This happened regularly in Israel, sporadically elsewhere. But even in the higher Paganism, I do not think this process

[1] faith seeking understanding.
[2] Rudolf Otto, *The Idea of the Holy*, trans. John W. Harvey (London, 1923).

led to anything exactly like *fides*. There is nothing credal in Paganism. In Israel we do get *fides* but this is always connected with certain historical affirmations. Faith is not simply in the numinous *Elohim*, nor even simply in the holy Jahweh, but in the God 'of our fathers', the God who called Abraham and brought Israel out of Egypt. In Christianity this historical element is strongly reaffirmed. The object of faith is at once the *ens entium*[1] of the philosophers, the Awful Mystery of Paganism, the Holy Law given of the moralists, and Jesus of Nazareth who was crucified under Pontius Pilate and rose again on the third day.

Thus we must admit that Faith, as we know it, does not flow from philosophical argument alone; nor from experience of the Numinous alone; nor from moral experience alone; nor from history alone; but from historical events which at once fulfil and transcend the moral category, which link themselves with the most numinous elements in Paganism, and which (as it seems to us) demand as their presupposition the existence of a Being who is more, but not less, than the God whom many reputable philosophers think they can establish.

Religious experience, as we know it, really involves all these elements. We may, however, use the word in a narrower sense to denote moments of mystical, or devotional, or merely numinous experience; and we may then ask, with Professor Price, how such moments, being a kind of *visio*, are related to faith, which by definition is 'not sight'. This does not seem to me one of the hardest questions. 'Religious experience' in the narrower sense comes and goes: especially goes. The operation of Faith is to retain, so far as the will and intellect are concerned, what is irresistible and obvious during the moments of special grace. By faith we believe always what we hope hereafter to see always and perfectly and have already seen imperfectly and by flashes. In relation to the

---

[1] being of beings.

philosophical premises a Christian's faith is of course excessive: in relation to what is sometimes shown him, it is perhaps just as often defective. My faith even in an earthly friend goes beyond all that could be demonstratively proved; yet in another sense I may often trust him less than he deserves.

21 Xmas and Christmas (1954)
A Lost Chapter from Herodotus

And beyond this there lies in the ocean, turned towards the west and north, the island of Niatirb which Hecataeus indeed declares to be the same size and shape as Sicily, but it is larger, though in calling it triangular a man would not miss the mark. It is densely inhabited by men who wear clothes not very different from the other barbarians who occupy the north-western parts of Europe though they do not agree with them in language. These islanders, surpassing all the men of whom we know in patience and endurance, use the following customs.

In the middle of winter when fogs and rains most abound they have a great festival which they call Exmas, and for fifty days they prepare for it in the fashion I shall describe. First of all, every citizen is obliged to send to each of his friends and relations a square piece of hard paper stamped with a picture, which in their speech is called an Exmas-card. But the pictures represent birds sitting on branches, or trees with a dark green prickly leaf, or else men in such garments as the Niatirbians believe that their ancestors wore two hundred years ago riding in coaches such as their ancestors used, or houses with snow on their roofs. And the Niatirbians are unwilling to say what these pictures have to do with the festival, guarding (as I suppose) some sacred mystery. And because all men must send these cards the marketplace is filled with the crowd of those buying them, so that there is great labour and weariness.

But having bought as many as they suppose to be sufficient, they return to their houses and find there the like cards which others have sent to them. And when they find cards from any to whom they also have sent cards, they throw them away and give thanks to the gods that this labour at least is over for another year. But when they find cards from any to whom they have not sent, then they beat their breasts and wail and utter curses against the sender; and, having sufficiently lamented their misfortune, they put on their boots again and go out into the fog and rain and buy a card for him also. And let this account suffice about Exmas-cards.

They also send gifts to one another, suffering the same things about the gifts as about the cards, or even worse. For every citizen has to guess the value of the gift which every friend will send to him so that he may send one of equal value, whether he can afford it or not. And they buy as gifts for one another such things as no man ever bought for himself. For the sellers, understanding the custom, put forth all kinds of trumpery, and whatever, being useless and ridiculous, they have been unable to sell throughout the year they now sell as an Exmas gift. And though the Niatirbians profess themselves to lack sufficient necessary things, such as metal, leather, wood and paper, yet an incredible quantity of these things is wasted every year, being made into the gifts.

But during these fifty days the oldest, poorest and most miserable of the citizens put on false beards and red robes and walk about the market-place; being disguised (in my opinion) as *Cronos*. And the sellers of gifts no less than the purchasers become pale and weary, because of the crowds and the fog, so that any man who came into a Niatirbian city at this season would think some great public calamity had fallen on Niatirb. This fifty days of preparation is called in their barbarian speech the Exmas *Rush*.

But when the day of the festival comes, then most of the citizens, being exhausted with the *Rush*, lie in bed till noon. But in the evening they eat five times as much supper as on other days and, crowning themselves with crowns of paper, they become intoxicated. And on the day after Exmas they are very grave, being internally disordered by the supper and the drinking and reckoning how much they have spent on gifts and on the wine. For wine is so dear among the Niatirbians that a man must swallow the worth of a talent before he is well intoxicated.

Such, then, are their customs about the Exmas. But the few among the Niatirbians have also a festival, separate and to themselves, called Crissmas, which is on the same day as Exmas. And those who keep Crissmas, doing the opposite to the majority of the Niatirbians, rise early on that day with shining faces and go before sunrise to certain temples where they partake of a sacred feast. And in most of the temples they set out images of a fair woman with a new-born Child on her knees and certain animals and shepherds adoring the Child. (The reason of these images is given in a certain sacred story which I know but do not repeat.)

But I myself conversed with a priest in one of these temples and asked him why they kept Crissmas on the same day as Exmas; for it appeared to me inconvenient. But the priest replied, It is not lawful, O Stranger, for us to change the date of Crissmas, but would that Zeus would put it into the minds of the Niatirbians to keep Exmas at some other time or not to keep it at all. For Exmas and the *Rush* distract the minds even of the few from sacred things. And we indeed are glad that men should make merry at Crissmas; but in Exmas there is no merriment left. And when I asked him why they endured the *Rush*, he replied, It is, O Stranger, a *racket*; using (as I suppose) the words of some oracle and speaking unintelligibly to me (for a *racket* is an instrument which the barbarians use in a game called *tennis*).

But what Hecataeus says, that Exmas and Crissmas are the same, is not credible. For first, the pictures which are stamped on the Exmas-cards have nothing to do with the sacred story which the priests tell about Crissmas. And secondly, the most part of

the Niatirbians, not believing the religion of the few, nevertheless send the gifts and cards and participate in the *Rush* and
drink, wearing paper caps. But it is not likely that men, even
being barbarians, should suffer so many and great things in honour of a god they do not believe in. And now, enough about
Niatirb.

22 Prudery and Philology (1955)

We have had a good deal of discussion lately about what is called obscenity in literature, and this discussion has (very naturally) dealt with it chiefly from a legal or moral point of view. But the subject also gives rise to a specifically literary problem.

There have been very few societies, though there have been some, in which it was considered shameful to make a drawing of the naked human body: a detailed, unexpurgated drawing which omits nothing that the eye can see. On the other hand, there have been very few societies in which it would have been permissible to give an equally detailed description of the same subject in words. What is the cause of this seemingly arbitrary discrimination?

Before attempting to answer that question, let us note that the mere existence of the discrimination disposes of one widely accepted error. It proves that the objection to much that is called 'obscenity' in literature is not exclusively moral. If it were, if the objectors were concerned merely to forbid what is likely to inflame appetite, the depicted nude should be as widely prohibited as the described nude. It might, indeed, be regarded as the more objectionable: *segnius irritant,* things seen move men more than things reported. No doubt, some books, and some pictures, have been censured on purely moral grounds, censured as 'inflammatory'. But I am not speaking of such special cases: I am speaking of the quite general concession to the artist of that which is denied to the writer. Something other than a care for chastity seems to be involved.

166

And fortunately there is a very easy way of finding out why the distinction exists. It is by experiment. Sit down and draw your nude. When you have finished it, take your pen and attempt the written description. Before you have finished you will be faced with a problem which simply did not exist while you were working at the picture. When you come to those parts of the body which are not usually mentioned, you will have to make a choice of vocabulary. And you will find that you have only four alternatives: a nursery word, an archaism, a word from the gutter, or a scientific word. You will not find any ordinary, neutral word, comparable to 'hand' or 'nose'. And this is going to be very troublesome. Whichever of the four words you choose is going to give a particular tone to your composition: willy-nilly you must produce baby-talk, or Wardour Street, or coarseness, or technical jargon. And each of these will force you to imply a particular attitude (which is not what you intended to imply) towards your material. The words will force you to write as if you thought it either childish, or quaint, or contemptible, or of purely scientific interest. In fact, *mere* description is impossible. Language forces you to an implicit comment. In the drawing you did not need to comment: you left the lines to speak for themselves. I am talking, of course, about mere draughtsmanship at its simplest level. A completed work by a real artist will certainly contain a comment about something. The point is that, when we use words instead of lines, there is really nothing that corresponds to mere draughtsmanship. The pen always does both less and more than the pencil.

This, by the by, is the most important of all facts about literature. There never was a falser maxim than *ut pictura poesis*. We are sometimes told that everything in the word can come into literature. This is perhaps true in some sense. But it is a dangerous truth unless we balance it with the statement that nothing can go into literature except words, or (if you prefer) that nothing can go in except by becoming words. And words, like every other medium, have their own proper powers and limitations. (They are, for instance, all but impotent when it comes to describing even the simplest machines. Who could, in words, explain what a screw, or a pair of scissors, is like?)

One of these limitations is that the common names (as distinct from the childish, archaic, or scientific names) for certain things are 'obscene' words. It is the words, not the things, that are obscene. That is, they are words long consecrated (or desecrated) to insult, derision, and buffoonery. You cannot use them without bringing in the whole atmosphere of the slum, the barrack-room, and the public school.

It may of course be said that this state of affairs – this lack of any neutral and straightforward words for certain things – is itself the result of precious prudery. Not, to be sure, of 'Victorian' or 'Puritan' prudery, as the ignorant say, but of a prudery certainly pre-Christian and probably primeval. (Quintilian on the 'indecencies' which his contemporaries found in Virgil is an eye-opener; no Victorian was ever so pruriently proper.) The modern writer, if he wishes to introduce into serious writing (comic works are a different matter) a total liberty for the pen such as has nearly always been allowed to the pencil, is in fact taking on a much more formidable adversary than a local (and, we may hope, temporary) state of English law. He is attempting to rip up the whole fabric of the mind. I do not say that success is impossible, still less that the attempt is perverse. But before we commit ourselves to so gigantic an enterprise, two questions seem to be worth asking.

First, is it worth it? Have good writers not better things to do? For of course the present state of the law, and (what is less easily utterable) of taste, cannot really prevent any writer worth his salt from saying, in effect, whatever he wants to say. I should insult the technical proficiency of our contemporaries if I supposed them so little masters of the medium as to be unable, whatever their theme, to evade the law. Many perhaps would feel such evasion to be disgraceful. Yet why? The contemporary state of sensibility is surely, like the language, part of the author's raw material. Evasion (I admit the word has a shabby sound) need not really be less creditable than the 'turning' of any other difficulty which one's medium presents. Great work can be done in a difficult metre; why not also under difficult restraints of another kind? When authors rail too much (we may allow them to rail a little) against public taste, do they perhaps betray some insufficiency? They denigrate what they ought rather to use and finally transform by first obeying.

Secondly, do we not stand to lose more than we gain? For of course to remove all 'prudery' is to remove one area of vivid sensibility, to expunge a human feeling. There are quite enough etiolated, inert, neutral words knocking about already: do we want to increase their number? A strict moralist might possibly argue that the old human reticence about some of our bodily functions has bred such mystery and prurience ('It is impossible', said the girl in Shaw, 'to explain decency without being indecent') that it cannot be abolished too soon. But would the strict moralist be right? Has nothing good come out of it? It is the parent of three-quarters of the world's jokes. Remove the standard of decency in the written word, and one of two results must follow. Either you can never laugh again at most of Aristophanes, Chaucer or Rabelais, the joke having partly depended on the fact that what is mentioned is unmentionable, or, horrid thought, the oral *fableau* as we have all heard it in taproom (not by any means always vile or prurient, but often full of true humour and traditional art) will be replaced and killed by written, professional *fableaux*: just as the parlour games we played for ourselves fifty years ago are now played for us by professionals 'on the air'. The smoking-room story is, I grant, the last and least of the folk-arts. But it is the only one we have left. Should not writers be willing to preserve it at the cost of a slight restraint on their own vocabulary?

23 Is History Bunk? (1957)

The historical impulse – curiosity about what men thought, did, and suffered in the past – though not universal, seems to be permanent. Different justifications have been found for the works which gratify it. A very simple one is that offered in Barbour's *Bruce*;[1] exciting stories are in any case 'delitabill' and if they happen to be true as well then we shall get a 'doubill pleasance'. More often graver motives are put forward. History is defended as instructive or exemplary: either ethically (the lasting fame or infamy which historians confer upon the dead will teach us to mind our morals) or politically (by seeing how national disasters were brought on in the past we may learn how to avoid them in the future).

As the study of history develops and becomes more like a science these justifications are less confidently advanced. Modern historians are not so ready to classify kings as 'good' and 'bad'. The lessons to be learned by statesmen from past errors becomes less obvious the more we know. The uniqueness of every historical situation stands out more clearly. In the end most of those who care about history find it safer and franker to admit that they are seeking knowledge of the past (as other men seek knowledge of the nebulae) for its own sake; that they are gratifying a 'liberal' curiosity.

[1] John Barbour (1316?–1395) composed his poem *The Bruce*, celebrating the war of independence and deeds of King Robert and James Douglas, about 1375.

171

The conception of a 'liberal' curiosity and of the 'liberal' studies which exist to satisfy it is one we owe to Aristotle. 'We call a man *free* whose life is lived for his own sake, not for that of others. In the same way philosophy is of all studies the only *free* one: because it alone exists for its own sake' *(Metaphysics* 982b). Of course *philosophy* does not here mean, as now, the rump or residuum left by the specialization of the various sciences. And perhaps Aristotle would not, in any case, have allowed the word to cover history (cf. *Poetics* 1451b). That hardly matters. In his conception of a study pursued not for some end beyond itself but for its own sake he has provided most of the activities we carry on at universities with their charter.

Of course this conception (Aristotle meant it only for freemen) has always been baffling and repellent to certain minds. There will always be people who think that any more astronomy than a ship's officer needs for navigation is a waste of time. There will always be those who, on discovering that history cannot really be turned to much practical account, will pronounce history to be Bunk. Aristotle would have called this servile or banausic; we, more civilly, may christen it Fordism.

As the study of history progresses it is almost inevitable, and surely not unreasonable, that partial or departmental histories should arise. The whole past, even within a limited period, becomes too large. Thus we get histories of particular human activities – of law, of shipbuilding, of clothes, of cookery, architecture, or literature. Their justification is the same as that of history *simpliciter* (which, after all, usually meant in effect the history of war and politics). They exist to gratify a liberal curiosity. The knowledge of how men dressed or built or wrote in the past, and why, and why they liked doing it that way, and what it felt like to like that sort of thing, is being sought for its own sake.

Clearly a Fordist view might be taken of these partial histories. It might be maintained that the history of law was legitimate in so far as it yielded practical results: that it studied, or ought to study, 'the valuable' and therefore should notice bad laws and unjust modes of trial only because, and in so far as, those taught us to appreciate more fully the practice of the Nineteenth Century and therefore to resist more obstinately what seems likely to come upon us in the latter part of the Twentieth. This of course is a worthy object. But the claim that legal history depends for its whole right to exist on the performance of such a *corvée* will be granted only by a thorough-going Fordist. We others feel that we should like to know and understand the legal behaviour and legal thought of our ancestors even if no practical gains follow from it.

The departmental history which seems most liable to such attack just at present is the history of literature. Mr Mason said recently in the *Review*, 'it is the study of what is valuable; study of minor figures is only justified if it contributes to the understanding of what is meant by *major*'.[1] Now of course, if we grant that the discipline of literary history is, or can be, or ought to be, merely ancillary to the art of literary criticism, we shall agree with Mr Mason. But why should we grant this?

Let us be quite clear what the question is. If a man says, 'I have no interest in the history of literature simply as history', one would have no controversy with him. One would reply, 'Well, I dare say not; don't let me detain you.' If he says, 'I think criticism twenty times more important than any knowledge of the past', one would say, 'No doubt that is quite a reasonable view.' If he said, 'Literary history is not criticism', I should heartily agree. That indeed is my point. The study of the forms and styles and sentiments of past literature, the attempt to understand how and why they evolved as they did, and (if possible) by

---

[1] H. A. Mason, 'Churchill's Satire', a review of *The Poetical Works of Charles Churchill*, ed. Douglas Grant (1956) in *The Cambridge Review*, vol. LXXVI-II (11 May 1957), p. 571.

a sort of instructed empathy to re-live momentarily in ourselves the tastes for which they catered, seems to me as legitimate and liberal as any other discipline; even to be one without which our knowledge of man will be very defective. Of course it is not a department of criticism; it is a department of a department of history *(Kulturgeschichte)*. As such it has its own standing. It is not to be judged by the use it may or may not happen to have for those whose interests are purely critical.

Of course I would grant (and so, I expect, would Mr Mason) that literary history and criticism can overlap. They usually do. Literary historians nearly always allow themselves some valuations, and literary critics nearly always commit themselves to some historical propositions. (To describe an element in Donne's poetry as new commits you to the historical proposition that it is not to be found in previous poetry.) And I would agree (if that is part of what he means) that this overlap creates a danger of confusions. Literary (like constitutional) historians can be betrayed into thinking that when they have traced the evolution of a thing they have somehow proved its worth; literary critics may be unaware of the historical implications (often risky) which lurk in their evaluative criticism.

But if Mr Mason is denying literary history's right to exist, if he is saying that no one must study the past of literature except as a means of criticism, I think his position is far from self-evident and ought to be supported. And I think he is denying that. For if one values literary history as history, it is of course very clear why we study bad work as well as good. To the literary historian a bad, though once popular, poem is a challenge; just as some apparently irrational institution is a challenge to the political historian. We want to know how such stuff came to be written and why it was applauded; we want to understand the whole *ethos* which made it attractive. We are, you see, interested in men. We do not demand that everyone should share our interests.

The whole question invites further discussion. But I think that discussion will have to begin further back. Aristotle's (or Newman's) whole conception of the liberal may have to be questioned. Fordism may admit of some brilliant defence. We may have to ask whether literary criticism is itself an end or a means and, if a means, to what. But till all this has been canvassed I was unwilling that the case for literary history should go by default. We cannot, pending a real discussion, let pass the assumption that this species of history, any more than others, is to be condemned unless it can deliver some sort of 'goods' for present use.

24 Willing Slaves of the Welfare State[1] (1958)

Progress means movement in a desired direction, and we do not all desire the same things for our species. In 'Possible Worlds'[2] Professor Haldane pictured a future in which Man, foreseeing that Earth would soon be uninhabitable, adapted himself for migration to Venus by drastically modifying his physiology and abandoning justice, pity and happiness. The desire here is for mere survival. Now I care far more *how* humanity lives than how long. Progress, for me, means increasing goodness and happiness of individual lives. For the species, as for each man, mere longevity seems to me a contemptible ideal.

I therefore go even further than C. P. Snow in removing the H-bomb from the centre of the picture. Like him, I am not certain whether if it killed one-third of us (the one-third I belong to), this would be a bad thing for the remainder; like him, I don't think it will kill us all. But suppose it did? As a Christian I take it for granted that human history will some day end; and I am offering Omniscience no advice as to the best date for that

[1] From the French Revolution to the outbreak of the First World War in 1914, it was generally assumed that progress in human affairs was not only possible but inevitable. Since then two terrible wars and the discovery of the hydrogen bomb have made men question this confident assumption. *The Observer* invited five well-known writers to give their answers to the following questions: 'Is man progressing today?' 'Is progress even possible?' This second article in the series is a reply to the opening article by C. P. Snow, 'Man in Society', *The Observer* (13th July, 1958).

[2] One essay in J. B. S. Haldane's *Possible Worlds and Other Essays* (London, 1927). See also 'The Last Judgement' in the same book.

consummation. I am more concerned by what the Bomb is doing already.

One meets young people who make the threat of it a reason for poisoning every pleasure and evading every duty in the present. Didn't they know that, Bomb or no Bomb, all men die (many in horrible ways)? There is no good moping and sulking about it.

Having removed what I think a red herring, I return to the real question. Are people becoming, or likely to become, better or happier? Obviously this allows only the most conjectural answer. Most individual experience (and there is no other kind) never gets into the news, let alone the history books; one has an imperfect grasp even of one's own. We are reduced to generalities. Even among these it is hard to strike a balance. Sir Charles enumerates many real ameliorations. Against these we must set Hiroshima, Black and Tans, Gestapo, Ogpu, brain-washing, the Russian slave camps. Perhaps we grow kinder to children; but then we grow less kind to the old. Any GP will tell you that even prosperous people refuse to look after their parents. 'Can't they be got into some sort of Home?' says Goneril.[1]

More useful, I think, than an attempt at balancing, is the reminder that most of these phenomena, good and bad, are made possible by two things. These two will probably determine most of what happens to us for some time.

The first is the advance, and increasing application, of science. As a means to the ends I care for, this is neutral. We shall grow able to cure, and to produce, more diseases – bacterial war, not bombs, might ring down the curtain – to alleviate, and to inflict, more pains, to husband, or to waste, the resources of the planet more extensively. We can become either more beneficent or more mischievous. My guess is that we shall do both; mending one thing and marring another, removing old miseries and producing

[1] In Shakespeare's *King Lear*.

new ones, safeguarding ourselves here and endangering ourselves there.

The second is the changed relation between Government and subjects. Sir Charles mentions our new attitude to crime. I will mention the trainloads of Jews delivered at the German gas-chambers. It seems shocking to suggest a common element, but I think one exists. On the humanitarian view all crime is pathological; it demands not retributive punishment but cure. This separates the criminal's treatment from the concepts of justice and desert; a 'just cure' is meaningless.

On the old view public opinion might protest against a punishment (it protested against our old penal code) as excessive, more than the man 'deserved'; an ethical question on which anyone might have an opinion. But a remedial treatment can be judged only by the probability of its success; a technical question on which only experts can speak. Thus the criminal ceases to be a person, a subject of rights and duties, and becomes merely an object on which society can work. And this is, in principle, how Hitler treated the Jews. They were objects; killed not for ill desert but because, on his theories, they were a disease in society. If society can mend, remake and unmake men at its pleasure, its pleasure may, of course, be humane or homicidal. The difference is important. But, either way, rulers have become owners.

Observe how the 'humane' attitude to crime could operate. If crimes are diseases, why should diseases be treated differently from crimes? And who but the experts can define disease? One school of psychology regards my religion as a neurosis. If this neurosis ever becomes inconvenient to Government, what is to prevent my being subjected to a compulsory 'cure'? It may be painful; treatments sometimes are. But it will be no use asking, 'What have I done to deserve this?' The Straightener will reply:

'But, my dear fellow, no one's *blaming* you. We no longer believe in retributive justice. We're healing you.'

This would be no more than an extreme application of the political philosophy implicit in most modern communities. It has stolen on us unawares. Two wars necessitated vast curtailments of liberty, and we have grown, though grumblingly, accustomed to our chains. The increasing complexity and precariousness of our economic life have forced Government to take over many spheres of activity once left to choice or chance. Our intellectuals have surrendered first to the slave-philosophy of Hegel, then to Marx, finally to the linguistic analysts.

As a result, classical political theory, with its Stoical, Christian and juristic key-conceptions (natural law, the value of the individual, the rights of man), has died. The modern State exists not to protect our rights but to do us good or make us good – anyway, to do something to us or to make us something. Hence the new name 'leaders' for those who were once 'rulers'. We are less their subjects than their wards, pupils, or domestic animals. There is nothing left of which we can say to them, 'Mind your own business.' Our whole lives *are* their business.

I write 'they' because it seems childish not to recognize that actual government is and always must be oligarchical. Our effective masters must be more than one and fewer than all. But the oligarchs begin to regard us in a new way.

Here, I think, lies our real dilemma. Probably we cannot, certainly we shall not, retrace our steps. We are tamed animals (some with kind, some with cruel, masters) and should probably starve if we got out of our cage. That is one horn of the dilemma. But in an increasingly planned society, how much of what I value can survive? That is the other horn.

I believe a man is happier, and happy in a richer way, if he has 'the freeborn mind'. But I doubt whether he can have this without economic independence, which the new society is abolishing.

For economic independence allows an education not controlled by Government; and in adult life it is the man who needs, and asks, nothing of the Government who can criticize its acts and snap his fingers at its ideology. Read Montaigne; that's the voice of a man with his legs under his own table, eating the mutton and turnips raised on his own land. Who will talk like that when the State is everyone's schoolmaster and employer? Admittedly, when man was untamed, such liberty belonged only to the few. I know. Hence the horrible suspicion that our only choice is between societies with few freemen and societies with none.

Again, the new oligarchy must more and more base its claim to plan us on its claim to knowledge. If we are to be mothered, mother must know best. This means they must increasingly rely on the advice of scientists, till in the end the politicians proper become merely the scientists' puppets. Technocracy is the form to which planned society must tend. Now I dread specialists in power because they are specialists speaking outside their special subjects. Let scientists tell us about sciences. But government involves questions about the good for man, and justice, and what things are worth having at what price; and on these a scientific training gives a man's opinion no added value. Let the doctor tell me I shall die unless I do so-and-so; but whether life is worth having on those terms is no more a question for him than for any other man.

Thirdly, I do not like the pretensions of Government – the grounds on which it demands my obedience – to be pitched too high. I don't like the medicine man's magical pretensions nor the Bourbon's Divine Right. This is not solely because I disbelieve in magic and in Bossuet's *Politique*.[1] I believe in God, but I detest theocracy. For every Government consists of mere men and is,

---

[1] Jacques Bénigne Bossuet, *Politique tirée des propres paroles de l'Écriture-Sainte* (Paris, 1709).

strictly viewed, a makeshift; if it adds to its commands 'Thus saith the Lord', it lies, and lies dangerously.

On just the same ground I dread government in the name of science. That is how tyrannies come in. In every age the men who want us under their thumb, if they have any sense, will put forward the particular pretension which the hopes and fears of that age render most potent. They 'cash in'. It has been magic, it has been Christianity. Now it will certainly be science. Perhaps the real scientists may not think much of the tyrants' 'science' – they didn't think much of Hitler's racial theories or Stalin's biology. But they can be muzzled.

We must give full weight to Sir Charles's reminder that millions in the East are still half starved. To these my fears would seem very unimportant. A hungry man thinks about food, not freedom. We must give full weight to the claim that nothing but science, and science globally applied, and therefore unprecedented Government controls, can produce full bellies and medical care for the whole human race: nothing, in short, but a world Welfare State. It is a full admission of these truths which impresses upon me the extreme peril of humanity at present.

We have on the one hand a desperate need: hunger, sickness and the dread of war. We have, on the other, the conception of something that might meet it: omnicompetent global technocracy. Are not these the ideal opportunity for enslavement? This is how it has entered before: a desperate need (real or apparent) in the one party, a power (real or apparent) to relieve it, in the other. In the ancient world individuals have sold themselves as slaves, in order to eat. So in society. Here is a witch-doctor who can save us from the sorcerers – a war-lord who can save us from the barbarians – a Church that can save us from Hell. Give them what they ask, give ourselves to them bound and blindfold, if only they will! Perhaps the terrible bargain will be made again.

We cannot blame men for making it. We can hardly wish them not to. Yet we can hardly bear that they should.

The question about progress has become the question whether we can discover any way of submitting to the world-wide paternalism of a technocracy without losing all the personal privacy and independence. Is there any possibility of getting the super Welfare State's honey and avoiding the sting?

Let us make no mistake about the sting. The Swedish sadness is only a foretaste. To live his life in his own way, to call his house his castle, to enjoy the fruits of his own labour, to educate his children as his conscience directs, to save for their prosperity after his death – these are wishes deeply ingrained in white and civilized man. Their realization is almost as necessary to our virtues as to our happiness. From their total frustration disastrous results, both moral and psychological, might follow.

All this threatens us even if the form of society which our needs point to should prove an unparalleled success. But is that certain? What assurance have we that our masters will or can keep the promise which induced us to sell ourselves? Let us not be deceived by phrases about 'Man taking charge of his own destiny'. All that can really happen is that some men will take charge of the destiny of the others. They will be simply men; none perfect; some greedy, cruel and dishonest. The more completely we are planned the more powerful they will be. Have we discovered some new reason why, this time, power should not corrupt as it has done before?

Original Sources

1. 'Why I Am Not a Pacifist' was read to a pacifist society in Oxford in 1940. Lewis made a copy of the manuscript for his former pupil and friend, George Sayer, and I have Mr Sayer to thank for providing me with a reproduction of it. The essay was included in an expanded edition of Lewis's *The Weight of Glory and Other Addresses* published by Macmillan Publishing Co. of New York in 1980. It was published for the first time in Great Britain in 1987 in *Timeless At Heart*.

2. 'Bulverism or, The Foundation of Twentieth-century Thought' is Lewis's title for the essay which appeared as 'Notes on the Way' in *Time and Tide*, vol. XXII (29 March 1941), p. 261.

3. 'First and Second Things' is the name Lewis gave this essay which first appeared as 'Notes on the Way' in *Time and Tide*, vol. XXIII (27 June 1942), pp. 519–20.

4. 'Equality' is reprinted from *The Spectator*, vol. CLXXI (27 August 1943), p. 192.

5. 'Three Kinds of Men' is reprinted from the *Sunday Times*, no. 6258 (21 March 1943), p. 2.

6. 'Horrid Red Things' was originally published in the *Church of England Newspaper*, vol. LI (6 October 1944), pp. 1–2.

7. 'Democratic Education' is Lewis's title for his 'Notes on the Way' from *Time and Tide*, vol. XXV (29 April 1944), pp. 369–70.

8. 'A Dream' is reprinted from *The Spectator*, vol. CLXXIII (28 July 1944), p. 77.

9. 'Is English Doomed?' is from *The Spectator*, vol. CLXXII (11 February 1944), p. 121.

10. 'Meditation in a Toolshed' is reprinted from the *Coventry Evening Telegraph* (17 July 1945), p. 4.

11. 'Hedonics' comes from *Time and Tide*, vol. XXVI (16 June 1945), pp. 494–5.

12. 'Christian Apologetics', published originally in *Undeceptions*, was read to an assembly of Anglican priests and youth leaders at the Carmarthen Conference for Youth Leaders and Junior Clergy during Easter 1945.

13. 'The Decline of Religion' is taken from an Oxford periodical, *The Cherwell*, vol. XXVI (29 November 1946), pp. 8–10.

14. 'Religion Without Dogma?' was read to the Socratic Society on 20 May 1946, and was published as 'A Christian Reply to Professor Price' in *The Phoenix Quarterly*, vol. I, no. 1 (Autumn 1946), pp. 31–44. It was then reprinted as 'Religion Without Dogma?' in *The Socratic Digest*, no. 4 (1948), pp. 82–94. The 'Reply' which I have appended to this essay is Lewis's answer to Miss G. E. M. Anscombe's article 'A Reply to Mr C. S. Lewis's Argument that "Naturalism is Self-refuting"', both of which appeared in issue no. 4 of *The Socratic Digest*. Those who are interested in Miss Anscombe's article will find it reprinted in her *Collected Philosophical Papers*, vol. II (1981).

15. 'Vivisection' appeared first as a pamphlet from the New England Anti-Vivisection Society (1947) and it was reprinted in this country by the National Anti-Vivisection Society (1948).

16. 'Modern Translations of the Bible' is my title for Lewis's Preface to J. B. Phillips's *Letters to Young Churches: A Translation of the New Testament Epistles* (Geoffrey Bles Ltd, 1947).

17. 'On Living in an Atomic Age' is taken from the last issue of

the annual magazine *Informed Reading*, vol. VI (1948), pp. 78–84.

18. I do not know which English publishers Lewis sent 'The Humanitarian Theory of Punishment' to. It was first published in *20th Century: An Australian Quarterly Review*, vol. III, no. 3 (1949), pp. 5–12. At the end of the essay Lewis added this postscript: 'One last word. You may ask why I send this to an Australian periodical. The reason is simple and perhaps worth recording: I can get no hearing for it in England.' The essay found a serious hearing in Australia and two criminologists, Norval Morris and Donald Buckle, published 'A Reply to C. S. Lewis' in *20th Century*, vol. VI, no. 2 (1952). After this Lewis's essay and Drs Morris and Buckle's 'Reply' were reprinted in the Australian law journal *Res Judicatae*, vol. VI (June 1953), pp. 224–30 and pp. 231–7. Then came J. J. C. Smart's 'Comment: The Humanitarian Theory of Punishment' in *Res Judicatae*, vol. VI (February 1954). This caused Lewis to write 'On Punishment: A Reply' – a reply to all three men – which was published in *Res Judicatae*, vol. VI (August 1954), pp. 519–23. Later, when Lewis allowed the English journal, *The Modern Churchman*, to reprint his original essay, he removed the postscript. It has since been reprinted in a number of American collections of essays on capital punishment and related issues. Of all Lewis's essays this is one of the most respected and certainly the most controversial. This book contains the original essay as well as Lewis's 'On Punishment: A Reply'.

19. 'The Pains of Animals: A Problem in Theology' originally appeared in *The Month*, vol. CLXXXIX (February 1950), pp. 95–104. I am very grateful to Miss M. F. Matthews for permission to include the late Dr C. E. M. Joad's part of this good-natured dispute.

20. 'Is Theism Important? A Reply' comes from *The Socratic Digest*, no. 5 (1952), pp. 48–51.

21. 'Xmas and Christmas: A Lost Chapter from Herodotus' was first published in *Time and Tide*, vol. XXXV (4 December 1954), p. 1607.

22. 'Prudery and Philology' is reprinted from *The Spectator*, vol. CXCIV (21 January 1955), pp. 63–4.

23. 'Is History Bunk?' is reprinted from *The Cambridge Review*, vol. LXXVIII (1 June 1957), pp. 647, 649.

24. 'Willing Slaves of the Welfare State' was originally published in *The Observer* (20 July 1958), p. 6.

Walter Hooper
Oxford